Herman Herst, Jr.'s

Still More Stories to Collect Stamps By

Published by
Mekeel's Weekly Stamp News
P.O. Box 5050
White Plains, NY 10602

ISBN 0-9635526-0-0

Preface

Preface. Whenever I see that word, my mind goes back to my third grade in elementary school when a teacher, still worthy of a blessing, told me that based on my juvenile ability then, I might someday be a successful writer.

The association with the word heading this page brings her to mind because she told me that most good books started with a preface. And so that we would never forget how to spell the word, she supplied the class with a mnemonic for it... Peter Rice Eats Fish And Catches Eels. I have never forgotten it.

It was in 1891 that a collector-dealer named C. H. Mekeel was confident that philatelists would support a weekly stamp newspaper, and backed up that confidence by starting Mekeel's Weekly Stamp News. Today, more than a century later, the magazine still appears regularly, never having missed a single issue in all those years.

Over the years, Mekeel's published some of the most useful books that today represent the core of philatelic literature. Some of philately's greatest students, philatelists such as August Dietz, B. W. H. Poole, Stanley B. Ashbrook, Murray Bartels, L. N. & M. Williams, Dr. Carroll Chase, F. Van Dyk MacBride, Elliott Perry, Mortimer Neinken, Creighton C. Hart, Edward N. Sampson, Ernest A. Kehr, George W. Brett, Barbara R. Mueller, Charles A. Fricke and Susan McDonald, all wrote for Mekeel's.

It is indeed an honor to have my name in such august company, and I want to thank Mekeel's for bringing to philately my thirteenth book on stamp collecting. May it bring to its readers what the writer has always felt to be philately's greatest reward...pleasure.

Herman Herst, Jr.

Introduction

Mekeel's is pleased to present to you *Still More Stories To Collect Stamps By.*

The most remarkable thing about this book is that it was written at all, for there was a time not too long ago when it appeared that Pat Herst's writing days...perhaps even his life...were threatened by debilitating illness. Instead, following a near miraculous improvement in his health, Herman Herst, Jr. continues to reign as the most prolific and best known philatelic writer of our time.

This, the thirteenth book by Pat Herst, is a compendium of some of his finest columns, some brand new, others previously published and revised. To the extent that we were starting from previously published articles, we acknowledge our compatriots at Canadian Stamp News, Linn's Stamp News, Stamp Collector, and Stamps for granting Pat Herst permission to publish them here in book form.

In editing *Still More Stories To Collect Stamps By*, I elected to treat each chapter as if it were brand new (for indeed all were new to me). Data that may have been outdated was brought up to the present, and statements were double-checked with Pat Herst to make certain they still were accurate. Given the personal or anecdotal nature of the material, any errors that may have slipped through will not affect your great enjoyment of *Still More Stories To Collect Stamps By.*

Beyond such fact checks, it would be presumptuous to think that anyone could improve on Pat Herst's rich and colorful writing, so we focused instead on the introduction of photographs and other illustrations to set this book apart from all the others. Because of my great admiration for Herman Herst, Jr., my mission was to try to make this the finest Herst book ever published. I leave it to literary critics and other readers to decide if we have succeeded. I can only give thanks that we were able to present this book to philately, and hope that there will be many more to come.

John F. Dunn,
Editor

Fondly dedicated to Miss Gulick, my third grade teacher, who wrote on my report card, "You show great imagination in your writing, and with your correct spelling and proper grammar, some day you should be a great writer."

Contents

1   How I Started As A Philatelist

We all started in different ways. My incentive was the stamp collection of my father, who died just after my fourth birthday.

When I was about seven my mother let me look at my father's collection. I was impressed with the great number of early revenues—almost every space in the album was filled. My father was a lawyer, and he must have developed a great source for revenue stamps.

"If you start a collection and stick to it for a year, you will get your father's collection," my mother told me. I plunged right in, bought an album, and instead of buying candy, I bought dime store stamp packets. I never developed a taste for sweets, even to this day.

The year went by and we went to the store room in the apartment house where we then lived. The collection had been stolen along with other things my mother had put away.

Years passed, and I continued my own collection. I started a stamp club at Lincoln High School in Portland, Oregon, where I then resided. Saturdays I went to work at a stamp store at 16th and Flanders Streets in Portland, and took my pay in stamps for my collection. I had little cash to buy stamps, but in 1925 when the Norse-American stamps appeared, I went to the Glisan Street Post Office and bought a full sheet for $2.00.

The letter rate was 2¢ at the time, and whenever I needed a stamp, I invaded that sheet. My philatelic knowledge was on a par with that of my goldfish, and I attacked that sheet at the top, where the plate number block was.

I came to New York to seek my fortune in 1933, and found a job in Wall Street delivering bonds. Wall Street and Nassau Street cross each other, and on my deliveries I passed the windows of the dozens of stamp dealers who had shops at the time. On a starting salary of $15 per week I did not have too much money for stamps, but I cut down on lunches and could indulge. (A firm called Nedick's had an "early bird" lunch before 11:30, consisting of frankfurter and roll, orange juice and coffee for fifteen cents.)

One of my deliveries was to Henry Needham, a well fixed investor who even in the depression was buying municipal bonds $25,000 and $50,000 at a time. Needham had on his wall sixteen large envelopes, under glass in a frame, arranged like a playing card hand, each with a Columbian stamp on it, from the one cent to the $5.00. Seeing that I admired it, Needham asked me if I collected. I told him that I did.

One day when I came to his office, he was affixing 1901 Pan-American stamps to a cover from a set of sheets that he had broken up. I was shocked at seeing these unhinged beauties going on an envelope, but he told me that when he wrote to collectors, he liked to make the envelope pretty. He asked if I owned any Pan-Americans and I replied in the negative. He removed a set of singles and gave them to me. "Never put anything in your album unless it is in perfect condition," he said. It was my first lesson in centering.

Another time Needham asked me what would be my greatest desire in the way of a stamp. I told him I would love a $5 Columbian. He asked me if I could pay $5 a week towards one. I replied that that would be impossible, but I might find a dollar a week. The next time I came in he showed me a beautiful used $5 Columbian. "It will cost you $12," he said. "I bought it for you in a Mozian auction. Enjoy it and give me a dollar a week."

It was a wonderful feeling to put it in my album. Had anyone seen my collection when I mounted it, it would have been unusual to see on that page a one cent and two cent Columbian and at the bottom of the page a $5 Columbian, the latter in even better condition than the two low values.

Every New York daily paper had a weekly column on stamps, on either Saturday, or Sunday if the paper was published on that day. Largest was the Evening Sun, which at its height was edited by the late Franklin Bruns. Among other things in the papers besides ads and stamp stories was a listing of stamp clubs.

There were dozens of clubs, and they met almost every night in the week. I lived on West 72nd Street, and the nearest club was the Empire State which met at the Hotel Lucerne on West 79th Street. Dues were $2 per year, a sum I could easily spare, for by 1934 my salary had reached $25 per week.

By then I had graduated from a Scott Imperial Album to the Scott International Junior. Just how albums could be produced for so little is still a mystery. The Imperial which held about 10,000 stamps with photos of many cheap ones sold for 35¢—and that included the profit that the dealer made on it. The International Junior was clothbound and held 35,000 stamps. It sold for $3.25. Everything that looked like a stamp went into the album. Christmas seals, labels, revenues and tax stamps found their way into it. Pages were ringed by stamps of that particular country which were not postage stamps.

Slowly my stamp collection grew. One could buy a packet of 500 stamps for a dollar. The only trouble was that pages facing each other would have the stamps tangled. I learned how to place a sheet of stationery between each double page. It fattened the album but it preserved the stamps.

Each summer I had my work cut out for me. A new album from Scott for another $3.25 had to be used with stamps moved from the old one. I blessed the peelable hinges; in my earlier days I had used transparent mending tissue that librarians used to patch torn pages. Stamps mounted with that stuck like cast iron.

Once all the stamps were placed in the new album, it

became time for the census, with all the stamps counted. The labels and revenues were included in the total. The album had spaces for 35,000 stamps, true, but I could not seem to get past the 5,000 mark. And had you asked me to guess the value, I would come up with a figure based more on fond wishes than on an actual count.

My first lesson at the Empire State was a hard one to learn. "Don't waste a hinge on a damaged stamp," a member told me. It was a harsh bit of advice, my album had many dozens of stamps with pieces out of them, or other defects. In my youthful haste years, to get them off letters and into my albums, I had not had the patience to soak them in water. I peeled them off. I was still penciling inside the front cover the number of stamps in the album, and it was a sad day when the number decreased by at least a tenth. I had to learn it simply is not true that half a stamp is better than no stamp at all.

A small group of postal employees from four of New York's boroughs started their own stamp club, but membership was not confined to post office people. Its convenient meeting location, a block or two from Gimbel's and Macy's, was a drawing card. It met at a cafeteria called Park's, on an upstairs balcony which was not needed during the evening. The proprietors made no charge for the meeting place; they only expected that occasionally a collector would spend a nickel for a cup of coffee.

In the 1930's, women were not welcomed in most of the more prestigious stamp clubs, so they started their own. (The Empire State was one of the few that did welcome them.) The ladies met at what later became one of New York's most expensive French restaurants, Copain, on 50th Street near First Avenue. It was a French restaurant even then, but at that time the proprietors offered their facilities free, again with the hope that someone might buy coffee.

The incredible thing in the Depression was the manner in which one could build a creditable collection without spending much money. We recall a collector of used air mail stamps, Sam Rodvien (who boasted one of the nation's finest collections of the then most popular specialty in stampdom), telling us that he had built his formidable collection almost

4

exclusively by swapping with other collectors.

Commemoratives were coming out with alarming frequency in the 1930s, and many post offices still had stocks going back to the days of the two-cent reds. At the All-Boro club particularly, the postal employees had access to plate blocks which sold in the shops for as much as double the face value. One could swap on a face value basis. I recall when a member came in with a half dozen plate number blocks of four of the 50¢ Graf Zeppelin which he exchanged for some 10¢ Washington Bicentennial plate blocks. (One reason for the relative scarcity of the 50¢ Graf Zeppelin in plate number blocks of six is the fact that given a choice between spending $2 and $3 for a plate block, most purchasers chose the former.)

The Bronx County Stamp Club was the largest club in New York in Depression days, and the "big operators" concentrated their attention there. The Club met at a hall on 149th Street in the Bronx. There were several long tables at which the members sat, and from 7:00 P.M. until midnight it was the philatelic center of the continent. (No female ever graced the room. Whether or not they might be admitted was never even discussed; it was just unthinkable.) One table was reserved for cash transactions; all of the others were restricted to swapping. The "cash table" was prophetically called the "dealers' table," prophetic because dozens of collectors first found there the realization of a desire to turn their hobby into a means of earning money. The Depression did this to many people who were out of work. We can think of at least two dozen members who became prominent philatelic professionals in the course of the next several decades.

The Third International Philatelic Exhibition (TIPEX), held at Grand Central Palace in New York in 1936, gave stamp collecting a degree of respectability previously unknown. A stamp collecting President, Franklin D. Roosevelt, and a stamp collecting king, George V of England, as well as the kings of Romania and Spain, finally convinced the average citizen that this was not a child's hobby, to be discarded as the wisdom of adulthood sets in.

At TIPEX, over 100,000 persons saw the world's finest collections. It was the "last hurrah" of dozens of wealthy men who had started collecting before the turn of the century, when a thousand dollars was a fantastic price to pay for a stamp. A few wealthy men guaranteed the expenses of the show. The New York press cooperated. Hundreds, maybe thousands, walked into the show as curious onlookers, and emerged as determined stamp collectors.

I was one of the "guides" at the show. One of the "curious" I showed around the exhibits introduced himself as John F. Rider, publisher of the Rider manuals, without which no radio repairman could exist, since it showed the circuits of every radio as soon as it hit the market. Rider, later known as the "Colonel" (his World War II rank), went on from that visit to become one of the nation's outstanding philatelists, with international gold medals to his credit for his collections of Lombardy-Venetia and Chile, among others.

Philatelic speculation has always been with us. Hundreds of collectors lost fortunes when they purchased quantities of the Columbian exposition issue in 1893; as late as 1920, they could not get even face value for their stamps, the high dollar values being particularly subject to discount. But TIPEX really woke up thousands to the possibilities of making money in stamps, and the small TIPEX souvenir sheet was the outstanding vehicle towards substantial profits. The face value was only twelve cents; less than three million were issued.

The queues to buy the souvenir sheet were long, but collectors always seem to be blessed with a considerable amount of patience when waiting in line to buy stamps. Even the non-collecting public joined the lines; perhaps if they bought a sheet of stamps today, in twenty years it would pay for a college education!

Saturday afternoon was the day of the speculators along Nassau Street; by 1936, I had opened up a stamp office there at 116 Nassau Street, the building which at its height housed thirty or forty stamp firms. (It is curious that today most stamp shops do not even open on Saturdays; the five-day work week has so penetrated our lives that Saturdays are little different from Sundays in downtown New York.)

Each Saturday TIPEX hit new highs. Some stamp dealers

were making more money on Saturday than during the rest of the week. They could buy TIPEX from one delighted seller at 50¢ per sheet, or $50 per 100, and sell the lot to a waiting buyer at $60. And the speculation was not confined to TIPEX sheets. It carried into other imperforate souvenir sheets that Uncle Sam had issued in earlier years, the 1933 Century of Progress and Byrd, the 1934 3¢ and 1¢ Parks. Speculators loved the souvenir sheets; there was no problem with centering, for they were imperforate, and on three of the five, there was no gum problem. They had been issued without gum.

The prices soared. TIPEX hit a dollar, and such a vast amount of them came on the market that buyers disappeared, and the price dipped to $20 per 100. I recall being offered a huge holding of 500 sets of the 1¢ and 3¢ Chicago sheets at face value. I was unable to find a buyer. (The seller finally discounted them at a postage broker, who privately perforated them and regummed them and sold them at face value to a large user. The stamps still turn up in used condition, and the finder wonders why he cannot find these stamps, with their odd perforations, in the Scott Catalogue.)

Oddly, the White Plains sheets (Scott 630), issued in 1926 for an earlier International Exhibition, never took the speculators' fancy, due no doubt to the fact that with twelve rows of perforations, six in each direction, a perfectly centered sheet even then was a rarity. As late as 1935, most dealers were using the off-centered sheets for postage (today $325, unused, in Scott).

As the dark clouds of the Depression lifted and the millions of collectors across the nation began to find themselves with money in their pockets, stamp prices began to ascend, a trend which has continued to this day. Then came the war and its shortages, and money that would otherwise be spent on new cars, refrigerators, and vacations was diverted into stamps. This added to the number of collectors, and the consequent shrinking of the stamp supply. If stamp collecting can be said to have come of age in the Depression, it was the war years and the boom of the late 1940s and 1950s that brought philately to its full maturity.

But that's another story.

2   Value is in the Eye of the Beholder

It is a simple matter to estimate the value of most philatelic material, assuming, of course, that the person doing the valuing knows his business.

But what if the item in question is something whose value one does not recognize?

Let us put it another way.

We once had a three cent Canadian small Queen. It listed in the catalogue for about thirty-five cents at the time, and nine out of ten Canadian collectors examining it would guess that was its value.

I turned it upside down, and there was a perfect Kicking Mule cancel on it. Quite certainly, the letter to which the stamp was affixed was brought to Port Townsend, Washington, put in the post office there, and received the popular American marking. Suddenly the stamp was worth about twenty-five dollars.

The point I want to make is that the same stamp can be honestly valued at two prices or even more, depending on the knowledge that each person has of the particular stamp.

And, of course, I am leading up to a true story. I was once located in Shrub Oak, New York. The late Seymour Kaplan, one of our great postal history students, lived about two miles away, and he never failed to drop in at my office to see what goodies had come in the mail. As I made the cash offers on incoming items, they were put in a cabinet drawer to await the acceptance of the offer. Seymour would write his name on the outer envelope in which a desired cover might be, and if my offer was accepted, he would have first call on it.

One day a cover came in with a single one cent blue Franklin, Scott #24. It was postmarked Ogdensburg, New York and it was addressed to Prescott, Ontario. The stamp, unfortunately, had a damaged corner, but it was well centered, the cover was most attractive, and I offered twelve dollars for it. Seymour saw it and put his name on the envelope. In the next two weeks, each day he pulled it out and asked if it were time. After two weeks, I told him his patience was about to be rewarded, and I suggested a fair price for it would be $17.50. He asked to borrow the cover and said he knew a better way to sell it.

A month later Seymour came to my office and put two one hundred dollar bills on my desk. I asked what the money was for, and he said it was for the one cent 1857 cover with the damaged stamp that he had "borrowed" some weeks before. I pressed him for the story.

He had taken the cover to a prominent New York dealer in early U.S. covers. "Do you expect DeVolpi soon?" he asked the dealer. The dealer replied that DeVolpi's visits were not regular, but he was due any day.

"Show him this cover and tell him that the price is five hundred dollars.

The dealer examined the cover. "He'll never buy it. The stamp is damaged. It isn't even a ten dollar cover." "Do as I say," Seymour told him. "He'll buy it."

DeVolpi came in and was shown the cover. His eyes lit up. He put it in a billfold and simply said, "Send me a bill."

"You haven't even heard the price," the dealer said. "How do you know you want it?"

"I want it," DeVolpi replied. "Just send me a bill." The dealer gulped and finally got it out. "The price is five hundred dollars." DeVolpi did not blink. "Just send me a bill," he said.

I knew there was more to the story, so I let Seymour continue. He asked if I had the set of Ashbrook books on the One-cent 1851-1857. He knew just what page to turn to.

He read what Ashbrook had to say. For a limited time, there was a special rate for mail crossing the St. Lawrence river from post offices on either side of the river. Letters were given to the captain, who was obliged to carry them as long as the one cent "ferriage rate" was paid. Seymour continued to read, getting to the important part. "Stampless covers are known with the one cent ferriage rate," Ashbrook had written, "but no cover has ever been found showing the rate being paid with a stamp."

Ashbrook had not lived to learn that such a cover had been found. Seymour continued.

"I gave the dealer one hundred dollars for delivering the cover to DeVolpi. I figure you deserved two hundred dollars for finding it and I deserved the same sum for recognizing it."

It all seemed fair.

Now do you understand what I was trying to say? Here was a cover that may have been through many different philatelic hands in the more than a century since it crossed the St. Lawrence. It was a nice ten dollar cover, despite the damaged stamp.

I had never heard of the "ferriage rate"; the dealer who sold it to DeVolpi knew nothing of a "ferriage rate". But the moment it was recognized for the rarity that it was, thanks to Seymour Kaplan's quick eye and even quicker memory, it became a five hundred dollar cover...and cheap at that.

Isn't philately wonderful? And isn't postal history even more wonderful if one takes the trouble to learn something about it?

I am looking for more ferriage rate covers. Perhaps this article may locate another...masquerading as a ten dollar cover...waiting to be given its due.

3   Let's Talk About Errors

Did you ever wonder why the centering of the top value of the King George V "Admiral" stamps of Canada leaves so much to be desired?

Well into the 1930s, in fact, almost to 1940, the Financial Branch of the Post Office in Ottawa which catered to philatelists' needs, continued to offer this stamp for sale at face. The centering was uniformly atrocious.

Officials ignored the pleas of hundreds of collectors, who had been urged by columnists in stamp magazines to flood them with letters, suggesting that they be taken off sale. It did no good. The Ottawa officials continued to sell them until they finally sold out, even though by then other dollar value stamps had appeared and were being sold.

An anomaly occurred with the re-issuing of the 50¢ stamp of the same series in 1925. First printings of this stamp were made in the intense black, listed in Scott now as #120a. In 1925 the stamp was reissued, but this time in a brownish shade. For a time, the newly issued stamp brought a premium over the one that had been on sale for thirteen years, especially with rumors that it would be discontinued in favor of an entirely new issue.

This new issue did appear in 1928, and in 1929 the 50¢ "Bluenose" did replace the 50¢ King George V. But so many collectors and speculators loaded up on the 50¢ brown, anticipating a scarcity that never did materialize, that today the latter catalogues at only $24.00 while the one-time much more common black shade lists at $45.00.

Speculators may attempt to tamper with the laws of supply and demand when it comes to stamps, but often not for long. Sooner or later, things stabilize, and the stamp that collectors thought would be the scarcer turns out to be the more common one.

There is a choice example of this in the stamps of New Zealand. In 1898, that country issued a set of pictorial stamps. The 2 1/2d value showed one of the Shaky Islands' famous scenes, Lake Wakatipu. Unfortunately, the engraver misspelled the name of the lake, and it appeared as Lake Wakitipu. Tremendous publicity resulted, and collectors besieged the post office for examples of the stamp with the error.

Shamefacedly, the Post Office reissued the stamp, with the lake's name properly spelled. Of course, no one wanted the corrected version. That would end up being the common one, everyone thought, and it was neglected. Everyone bet on the error.

It is not difficult to guess what happened. Turn to the New Zealand listings in Scott for Nos. 73 and 74. The more common of the two stamps is the error; the higher mint catalogue value is for the corrected stamp, which the speculators neglected to buy.

Are errors always valuable?

Now you know. As we hear so often when we ask what would seem to be a logical question, it all depends...

4 Katmandu Diary

Some years ago, INDIPEX was held in New Delhi, and the late Don Haverbeck and I were on the panel of judges. I always had a desire to visit Katmandu, the capital of Nepal, and since it was likely I might never have a better opportunity, Mrs. Herst and I made the short flight to this beautiful city in the Himalayas where roses bloom all year, despite its altitude, because of warm winds from the south and mountains that protect it from the cold of the north.

The first evening, after getting settled at the Crystal Hotel, in the center of Katmandu, we went for a walk in order to get the feel of the city. We had not gone more than a hundred feet when a young lad came to us, repeating over and over, "You need guide, mister?"

We really intended to see the city the next day, which we were to spend with a philatelic friend, Brihispati. (The Nepalese seem to get along very nicely with single names.) But as the boy pointed out Royal Palace, the Public Baths, and the mountain Swayanbu, (where Buddha is reputed to have been born) we accepted his offer.

Back at the hotel, our "guide" looked up and said "Mister, you do favor? Buy me dictionary." We had not seen a bookstore, but the boy knew where one was. We walked there, and I asked the bookseller to give the lad a dictionary, and we paid $2 for it.

The boy was in ecstasy. With tears in his eyes, he clasped my legs uttering thank you after thank you, and repeating "Now I learn English and be real guide."

We went to bed with a wonderful feeling, even remarking what happiness can be bought for such a nominal sum.

The next afternoon after our visit with Brihispati, on our way back to the hotel we met Don Haverbeck. Neither of us had known that the other would be visiting Katmandu after INDIPEX. We made a date for dinner at a popular restaurant, the Abominable Snowman. We did not see the Snowman, but did have a nice dinner. In the course of it, Don remarked "Let me tell you of the good deed we did on our way here this evening. A Nepalese youngster came up to us and asked us to buy him a dictionary so that he could learn English. You cannot imagine how grateful the youngster was."

I told Don that I really did not have to imagine it.

I have often wondered how many times that bookseller had sold what was probably the only English-Nepalese dictionary he had in stock. After all, he did not need more than one to do a thriving business.

And I doubt that the kid's English has improved from that day to this. He probably never held the dictionary long enough to open it.

5 The Original "Ponzi" Schemer

He was born Charles Ponsi in a small town in Italy in 1883. While still a boy, he changed the spelling of his last name to Ponzi, thus giving a new word to the language, one that has since become synonymous with confidence man. What is little known is that Ponzi's fortune was built on a mountain of International Reply Coupons, those small slips of paper that are still used by philatelic correspondents.

His family was a respectable one. His father was a baker, while his mother ran the home, taking care of his brothers and sisters. Charles received a good religious education, although right from his earliest years he was always in trouble with the priests and nuns for disobedience. His first arrest was when he was ten; he acted as lookout while a confederate stole some money from the cash drawer in a shop. The police searched his home and, to the consternation of his parents, they found, under some loose floorboards, the loot that the two boys had been stealing from stores in the village.

Ponzi was not the type of thief who broke into stores and homes. His specialty was to steal from folks whose carelessness made them vulnerable to being robbed. If he saw coins on a newsstand or an unguarded church poorbox, he simply appropriated the money. When a priest left money in a cassock he had removed, Ponzi emptied it. His father and mother were not exempt from his thieving fingers; any household money left loose soon vanished.

By the time he was sixteen, he found new avenues of opportunity in a gambling club. He soon realized that he had a fascination for cards. The locals were no match for his quick mind and adept fingers, and he found that cheating at cards provided a steady income without the risk of police interference. When he learned that for as little as thirty-five dollars he could buy steerage passage to America, he made a decision to seek his fortune abroad.

Alas, he learned that his fellow passengers were considerably more adept at cards than he was, and when he arrived in New York, the two hundred fifty dollars in Italian lira that he had left home with was reduced to two dollars. New York was not good to him. He refused all offers of employment, living from garbage cans and sleeping where he happened to be. Finally, to stave off starvation, he took a job in a restaurant on lower Broadway, and devoted himself to learning a new language. He saved his money and his first purchase was a dress suit so that he might become a waiter.

By altering patrons' restaurant bills and giving incorrect change, he supplemented his meager income. Concluding that New York did not offer him the opportunities that he had expected, he decided to go to Montreal. He had by now become quite proficient in English, so he applied for and successfully obtained a position in the Zrossi Bank, patronized by Italians, thus making his bilingualism a substantial asset.

The sight of all that money circulating around him gave Ponzi a desire to participate. The bank was pleased with his ability and he was given more and more authority. Before long, he became interested in three special accounts, each of which had a considerable number of entries with large balances. One account really excited him, that of a wealthy lady with a financial secretary who each day made out a batch of checks, which she signed without question.

Ponzi discovered an ability that he did not know he possessed: forgery. He practiced signing the lady's name, learning that if he did it upside down it looked more credible than otherwise. When a new chequebook was issued to the account, he appropriated several cheques. At this point he became greedy, and attempted to cash a cheque at the desk of an officer. The bank auditors caught Ponzi red-handed; he was rewarded with three years in prison, an event that made him decide he would be more careful in the future.

With a prison sentence behind, employment would be more difficult, and he felt that a return to the United States would assure him greater possibilities to use his gifts profitably.

He found employment with an import-export firm, J.P. Poole & Company of Boston. He applied himself to learning the business, hoping to find a niche for himself that would help him strike it rich. It was in this job that an event occurred that literally changed his life. A letter from Spain bore something he had never seen, an international reply coupon. International reply coupons, which are still available, were provided by the Universal Postal Union in 1906, to allow correspondents in one country to enable those in another country to reply to the letter. One simply bought a coupon at his own post office, sent it with his letter, and the recipient took it to his post office where it could be exchanged for a stamp of sufficient value to prepay the return postage.

The device fascinated Ponzi, especially when he went to the Boston post office and was given a five cent stamp for each coupon. He asked a Spanish friend what the coupons had cost. Spain, at that time, was enjoying what was the lowest postage rate in the world; the coupon was for sale there at one cent each. The possibilities, Ponzi realized, were limitless. If he could buy a huge supply of Spanish coupons at one cent each, and cash them for five times that, he would be able to sell them at four cents each, or twenty percent below the face value, and still quadruple his money.

He did not keep the idea a secret. It was legal in all respects, and he solicited investments from friends and fellow employees at Poole's. He had his first client on December 20, 1919, taking in two hundred and fifty dollars with which he was to buy coupons. His slogan was "50% profit in 45 days, double it in six months."

A good thing like this could not be kept quiet. Ponzi opened offices on School Street in Boston with luxurious mahogany furniture and bank-like grills. As a newspaper of the time wrote at the end of the scheme: "From Boston, all over the States, the good news was whispered. The local stream of investors turned into a nationwide torrent. Clerks, typists, secretaries, laborers, craftsmen, shopkeepers, small businessmen, all rushed to put their money into this new, wonderful idea." He even had a name for the enterprise: he called it the Securities Exchange Company.

By the spring of 1920, a quarter of a million dollars a week was rolling into his office. The queues in the street were so long that Ponzi hired girls to serve coffee and cake while investors waited their turn. His staff grew to sixteen clerks just to take in the money, with his chief assistant, an ex-butcher, earning seven thousand dollars a week. To get cash, many investors mortgaged their homes; Uncle Sam voiced displeasure that so many people were cashing their Liberty Bonds to obtain funds.

Wealth came easily to this Italian immigrant. He bought a controlling interest in a Boston bank, the Hanover Trust Company, and out of sentiment he bought Poole & Company outright. He bought a home, built by a millionaire, just outside Boston, with a heated swimming pool, a novelty of the day. Interior decorators charged him half a million dollars to make the home livable. One hundred thousand dollars went to stock his wine cellar, with clarets and brandies from the 1870s. He had a house staff of fifteen employees, including armed guards with orders to shoot any prowler on sight. The twenty acre estate was surrounded by a brick wall topped with barbed wire. His chauffeurs wore resplendent uniforms to match the expensive imported limousines he traveled in. Wherever he went, he was mobbed by people who cheered the success of this Italian immigrant whom America had made so wealthy. Ponzi's activities did not escape the notice of financiers. In an interview with a reporter, he said, "I buy millions of coupons and my scheme can be done by anyone except for one little thing—how I exchange these coupons for cash in America is my own secret."

Some investors suspected that Ponzi had a secret arrangement with the Post Office to redeem the coupons for cash, something that the Post Office insisted could not happen. Just what he was doing with the coupons was not one of Ponzi's worries, for he was in fact not buying them. The U.S. Post Office made its own investigation, and it learned that fewer than one million dollars worth of coupons had been cashed since Ponzi ostensibly started dealing in them. Confronted by this statement, Ponzi did not lose his composure.

"I have just used this postal coupon idea as a blind. I did not want the Wall Street boys to get even a hint of what my real scheme is. And so long as my depositors get back their investments with a profit, I do not have to account to anybody."

A run started in School Street and anxious investors clamored for their money. Ponzi had plenty of cash to meet all demands; as his clients walked out of the office counting new currency, the run soon stopped, and it changed to a queue of people wishing to invest their money. Many who had accepted refunds sought to reinvest. The Boston Post stated that investors gave Ponzi another five million dollars as a result of the rumors. Several attorneys offered their services to Ponzi in the event that he wished to sue the Post.

Ponzi's undoing came about as the result of an investigation of his Canadian activities. The Zrossis in Montreal identified Ponzi as the employee who had served three years in prison as the result of his theft there. Federal agents, armed with a warrant, entered Ponzi's School Street office, meeting unexpected resistance from investors waiting to leave money there. "Kill them!" was the greeting that the Federal agents received. His records, inadequate though they were, disclosed that he had taken fifteen million dollars from his investors. About one percent of that money was on hand in Ponzi's vaults, and this money the government took.

Ponzi pleaded guilty to the charge of embezzlement, and he was indicted on eighty-six counts of conversion. He received a sentence of five years in prison. One of his first purchases in prison was thousands of Christmas cards, which he laboriously addressed to each investor on the list that Uncle Sam gave him. The identical message on each card stated that he "regretted the recent miscarriage of our investments and hoped that it would not mar the spirit of Christmas. I look forward to stepping out of prison a free man at which time I will help you recover your losses." The response was unexpected. Some of his victims were so convinced of his honesty that they sent checks with their greetings, asking him to reinvest. These the authorities returned to the senders.

Ponzi served three and one half years' imprisonment, but the state of Massachusetts was not through with him. On his release, he was indicted for grand larceny. Twice the jury did not agree, and once a mistrial was declared. He was at last convicted again, and received a sentence of seven years. He was released in February 1934, to be greeted with jibes and insults from a waiting crowd, some of whom were undoubtedly the children of investors who had given him money fourteen years before. Thirty Boston police held back the threatening crowd, and drove Ponzi to a secret destination.

While he was in jail, prison officials realized for the first time that Ponzi had never become a U.S. citizen and he was back in jail when U.S. marshals arrested him for deportation proceedings. It was six months before he was put on a ship and taken back to Italy, some thirty-three years after his arrival in this country.

Once back in Italy, Ponzi used his abilities to inspire confidence, and he started a new career. He ingratiated himself with the Fascists and joined the Black Shirts. Mussolini was impressed with his savoir-faire and his linguistic abilities and he was sent to Rio de Janeiro to manage the office in Brazil for Alitalia, an Italian air line. He did such a fine job for his native country that for his sixtieth birthday he was given a testimonial dinner.

His job in Rio ended with Mussolini's downfall. Out of favor, along with all Fascists in Italy once Il Duce was hanged upside down with his mistress, Ponzi thought better of returning to Italy. On his own when the war ended, Ponzi became blind and a public charge. He died in Rio de Janeiro in January of 1949, at the age of sixty-six. A nun was at his bedside as he died.

His personal effects became the property of the Brazilian government. In his pockets was the total of his worldly possessions, sixty-two dollars and fifty cents in Brazilian money. It was just enough to pay for his funeral.

6   The Earliest Modern Local Post Cover

In late 1952, while writing on the private express companies, I chanced to read the Act of 1862, which permitted the establishment of private posts in areas that did not have local delivery. At the time, I resided in Shrub Oak, New York, in suburban Westchester County. I had an attorney write the Post Office, inquiring whether an individual might still set up a local post. I was happy to learn that one might, as long as the Post Office received the normal rate of postage in addition. Thus began the Shrub Oak Local Post. And for years, this writer basked in the confident knowledge, backed up by countless references, that he was the granddaddy of modern local posts.

It was in 1862 that mail was first delivered to certain homes and offices, but not everywhere. Until then, one visited the Post Office to pick up one's mail, or paid private companies to carry it to or from the Post Office. Even in 1952, ninety years after local delivery had started, it had not yet reached Shrub Oak.

With the Post Office closed Saturday and Sunday, there was no way for weekend visitors to the Shrub Oak resort area  to get their mail. Several families found the Shrub Oak Local Post useful, enabling them to get letters that otherwise would not have reached them. For years the post operated, with my two children acting as carriers, at two cents per letter. A triangular stamp was issued, picturing a mother oak, and two shrub oaks.

The Shrub Oak Local Post sparked dozens of posts all over the country, the majority of philatelic origin, but some filling a real postal demand. No one ever counted how many there were, but within a few years, there were hundreds. Some still operate today. There is even a society of collectors of modern local posts, the Local Post Collectors' Society, which produces a magazine called The Poster.

The first day of the Shrub Oak Local Post was May 1, 1953. Thousands of first day covers existed at one time, for my house organ, Herst's Outbursts, was mailed to all subscribers on that date. One wonders what happened to them; one of those covers sold for $24 in an auction not too long ago.

Nice as it is being a philatelic granddaddy, I must confess that the cover posted on May 1, 1953, was not the first modern day local post. That distinction goes to covers posted fourteen years before, at the 1939 New York World's Fair.

One of the popular exhibits at the World's Fair was Midget Town. It was a complete village, peopled by midgets, who day after day went about their business for the pleasure of the spectators. The village contained a church, a school, a bakery, private homes in which the midgets lived... and a working post office, completely separate from the United States Post Office. And the midgets issued a stamp.

Not only did they issue a stamp, but they had a last day ceremony, complete with a special postmark, when the Fair closed on October 27, 1940. Whether the stamps were available when the Fair opened on April 30, 1939, I do not know. Perhaps someone who collects philatelic souvenirs of the Fair will be able to tell us.

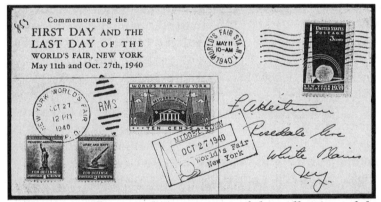

The cover illustrated is now part of the collection of the real doyen of local post collectors, Norman Williams, of London, brother of the late Maurice Williams, whose by-line "L. & M. Williams" has appeared over the years in so many magazines on both sides of the Atlantic. I was happy to present the cover to Mr. Williams in appreciation for his presenting me with a very scarce and as yet unidentified, local stamp picturing a polar bear, for my collection of polar bears on stamps.

7   Going, Going, Gone (Yesterday & Today)

The only light in the room was a flickering candle, so close to its final flicker that it would seem to have burned itself out, over and over. As the tiny wisp of flame seemed to rekindle the wick, one of the small group of men studying its action would utter a number. Then another, and another would state a higher number. And again the flame would seem to disappear completely, coming to life for a brief moment, during which bidding would resume. And then the flame died... completely.

When the flame died, the bidder who had given the last bid before the candle was finally extinguished congratulated himself, for his was the winning bid. Another tiny bit of candle was brought out, lit, and the procedure resumed, but with another item being sold. And it was in this manner that sales at auction were conducted many centuries ago.

In parts of the Orient, small objects, including stamps and coins, are sold at auction by a different means. The item to be sold is placed in a basket; the bidders sit in a circle, each bidder with a supply of small bits of paper, and a pencil. He examines the item being sold, writes a number on the slip of paper, drops it in the tray and passes it to the next person. If the latter wishes to bid, he does the same; if he does not, he simply passes the basket on, without bidding.

When the basket has completed the circle, the little bits of paper, each with a number and the initials or name of the bidder, are extracted and studied. The highest bid is called out and the person who made it is announced as the highest bidder. Each bidder has had but one opportunity to bid and his bid is, of course, the maximum that he is willing to pay. This is the method often used in Japanese stamp club auctions.

The Chinese auction operates in different fashion. Whether actually used in China is beside the point; many practices quite different from western procedures are simply given the "Chinese" appellation because they operate in a fashion different from that to which Westerners are accustomed.

In a Chinese auction, the item being sold is first examined by prospective bidders. The auctioneer then calls out a number, somewhat in excess of its actual value. When silence greets his call, he drops the figure slightly. Every few seconds, another number is called, and as the "non-bid" approaches the value of the object, tension in the room increases. Potential bidders know that they will have only one opportunity to bid on it and once the "auctioneer" gives a figure that a single bidder is willing to pay, the lot is knocked down. There is no second bid. In a Chinese auction, opportunity truly knocks but once.

And of course, there is a fourth method of selling at auction, the one known to all of us. Bidding is competitive. One may bid as often as he wishes, as long as there is an opposing bidder in the room. Once all competition is frightened away, the sole remaining bidder is declared the winner.

Common law, that body of law which is for the most part understood and underwritten in English-speaking civilizations, has a mass of rules pertaining to the sale of goods at auction. Ten centuries ago, when the poor peasant, possessed of little else but the clothes on his back and a few personal possessions, was unable to pay his debts or his taxes, his creditors had the right to seize anything of his belongings that suited their fancy, even his wife or children. There was literally nothing to protect him from those to whom he owed a debt, but the conscience of the creditors. More often than not, this was non-existent.

As common law developed, fundamental rights of the poor, the elderly and the friendless became a concern of government. Some of these were contained in the Magna Charta, that magnificent document forced on King John by his nobles; others were not reduced to writing, but developed over time, and today form the very foundation of British law. Among these, we recognize the right of a trial by a jury, composed of one's peers; the thesis that "man's home is his castle," forbidding forced entry without proper cause; and the right to recover, through prescribed means, property taken from him by debt.

Thus did auction enter into common law to enable the debtor to buy back property seized for debt, by providing that he might compete with others seeking to own it.

An entire body of law today surrounds sale by auction,

much of it at variance from ordinary business law. And this unwritten law today, many hundreds of years later, still is followed when an auction sale is conducted.

Abuses continued, despite laws made to protect the one who most needed protection. It is one thing to provide that all of a peasant's property was to be sold at auction, but if the auction were to be held in a secret place, knowledge of which was confined to but two or three people, it offered little protection to the unfortunate person whose goods were being sold. Auctions were held in the middle of a forest, in the dark of a moon, and only those in possession of the seized goods, and perhaps a few friends, were there to bid. Common law provides that the auction must be in a place of public assembly, that it be properly advertised, and that the unfortunate debtor whose goods were being sold must be given formal notice of where and when the sale would take place.

A red flag must be posted a prescribed distance from the venue of the sale. In the United States, this little bit of British common law has become American proper law in many places; a red flag visible to all within sighting distance must be posted at many country auctions. We have seen them as well at many stamp auctions where municipal or county or state law demands it.

But, of what use is a red flag posted on a dark night at the edge of a forest, or above a stone cave in a mountain? Common law provided that auction sales must be held in daylight. A red flag is useless if it cannot be seen. Even today, auction sales in New York, sponsored by an auctioneer with a New York city license, may be held only in daylight hours. One may hold a night sale, if one wishes, but it requires a special license for each individual night, at a cost over and above what the annual auctioneer's license costs, and in addition, one must place an advertisement in a "newspaper of public record" that such and such an auctioneer is planning a night sale.

That the sale itself should be held in a place of public assembly is a rather obvious and reasonable restriction. To hold a sale in a ladies' rest room might be a novelty, but since it is not a place of public assembly, it is doubtful that authorities would allow an auction sale to take place there. Similarly, common law dictates that there cannot be a charge levied to attend the sale, although this section of the law is frequently broken. Many auctions, run for charity, in order to discourage the curious and those least likely to buy, do make a charge to enter the room, a nominal five dollars or ten dollars, which, of course, goes to the charity in question. Others, aware of the law, do it a bit differently. They allow anyone in possession of the printed catalog to enter upon display of the catalog; one can obtain the catalog only through purchase.

Auction law and business law vary in many ways, not the least important of which is the matter of title. If one buys a glass mirror at a department store, and the store breaks it through its own negligence in delivery, the buyer is released from the obligation to buy it, or he may demand a replacement. But if he buys something at auction, and the auctioneer carelessly drops it before delivery, completely ruining it, the loss is the buyer's and not the auctioneer's. True, the right is seldom maintained, but common law decrees that title to the item passes to the owner at the drop of the hammer, even if the buyer has never as much as seen the item.

Admittedly, this little bit of common law is not often stressed, but nevertheless, it does exist—and if one were to study the terms of sale of some of the larger, more prestigious fine arts auction houses, it would be there, in black and white.

At a stamp auction held in connection with a major stamp exhibition in Los Angeles recently, a prospective bidder, desiring to examine the lots prior to the sale, was forced to pay a three dollar admission to the house where the lots were on view. He objected to the practice in letters to the editor in some American stamp magazines. He should instead have filed a complaint with the municipal authorities in Los Angeles, for it is quite possible that he has a valid complaint against the auctioneer and the ones running the show. (His complaint, he admits, was made solely on principle, for he claims to have spent more than three thousand dollars at the auction.)

No country in the world regulates stamp auctions more stringently than does the United Kingdom, which is not at all surprising when one recalls what a hopeless Pandora's box we might have without their steady vigilance. Posted on the wall in every auction room in Britain are warnings. Few perhaps read them, but almost all attending the sales understand them. The rules are intended to protect those whose material is being sold from various illegal acts which would serve to reduce the realization owners might expect from the sale of their material. The motives here are no different from those that insisted on a red flag and a daytime sale.

The most feared illegal operation at an auction is what is called the "knockout". In the United States, it is called a "ring". A ring consists of a group of potential bidders at an auction who have made an understanding that, at the sale itself, none will bid against another. The moment one member of the ring bids on a lot, all of the others remain silent. The result can be tragic for the owner.

At the sale's conclusions, each member of the ring picks up his lots and pays for them. They then retire to the office of one of them or to a motel room, if the sale should have been held in another city. Among themselves, they now have a REAL auction, each one bidding to the level he would have done in the auction room, had fair competition ensued.

At this second auction, a lot that may have sold for twelve dollars the first time, since it had no competition from ring members, might sell for forty dollars or more. Notes are made of the buyer of each lot and the price that was bid for it. When totaled, lots that at the first auction may have brought six hundred dollars in aggregate, will have brought perhaps eighteen hundred dollars at the second sale. Each successful buyer than picks up the lot on which he was the final buyer (even though he had not even bid on it the first time). For a lot on which he was willing to pay sixty dollars the first time (but which sold for twenty dollars) he now pays into the fund the twenty dollars at which price the lot originally sold. The auction house has been defrauded of sales of twelve hundred dollars; the owners of the stamps have suffered by a like amount.

It is quite apparent to anyone with experience attending a sale when an auction ring is operating. The mere fact that at no time during the sale does anyone note a member bidding against another is prime evidence. In Britain, it is the obligation of the auctioneer to make a complaint to the authorities.

This has been done, as recently as 1981, when a London ring was broken up and forbidden to try their tricks again. Punishment may vary from a fine to the denial of the right to bid in any auction for a specified time. Unfortunately, during almost fifty years of conducting auction sales in New York, the author knows of not a single instance when any action has been taken against a ring. They operate openly and they are most noticeable to the auctioneer crying the sale. In one instance, the writer noticed a ring operating, one of whose members was the auctioneer himself! The auctioneer was never again hired by the auction house for its sales.

In America, even more prevalent than the "knockout" is the "odds-evens" or "heads or tails" system. This system can only be used by two bidders, but when the two are most likely to be competitors, it can cost the auction house and the owners of the lots a considerable sum.

The two conspirators need not even sit near each other, and there need be no visible connivance with each other. Before the sale, the two simply agree that, as the sale progresses and bargains turn up, they will alternate bidding. It is not a ring, for each sale is final. What has happened is that each has agreed not to bid against the other. The modus operandi is simplicity itself. Bidder A will bid on any cheap lot that is an even number; Bidder B will bid only on the odd ones. Of course, they need to watch each other, for if Bidder A declines to bid on a cheap even numbered lot, there is no reason why Bidder B may not bid on it. A simple variation of "odd-even" is "heads-tails". Each bidder, A and B, has a coin before him, one with heads up, the other with tails. Once he has bought a lot, he reverses the coin, the "tails" side thus telling him that his fellow conspirator's turn has come.

There are unscrupulous uses made of auction procedure, especially in the case of items seldom sold on which a price level needs to be established. This can be done with the auction house entirely oblivious to the whole scheme. A collector has recently found a sheet of stamps with a recognizable error on it and he wishes to sell one at auction in order to determine what the actual market value is. He consigns the stamp to an auction house. The auction house accepts it, lists it and assigns what it feels to be a fair estimate of value, let us say thirty dollars. However, the owner of the stamp feels that the estimate is too modest. He would much rather see it bring eighty dollars.

This can be easily done. All he needs to do is ask two of his friends to place book bids on it, one perhaps at seventy dollars, another at seventy-five dollars. He asks a third friend to attend the sale and, when the lot opens at seventy-two dollars and fifty cents, he carries the bidding upwards, with the auctioneer obliging until the latter's highest book bid of seventy-five dollars is reached. The room bidder's hand is still upraised; he wins the lot for eighty dollars. He accepts the lot and pays for it. (The buyer, of course, also pays the usual ten percent premium, eight dollars, on his purchase, assuming that it was one of the auction houses that charges ten percent each to buyer and seller.)

He then returns the stamp to his friend, who reimburses him the eighty-eight dollars that he has paid the auctioneer. The auctioneer ultimately pays the owner the seventy-two dollars that he has coming, i.e. the realized price of eighty dollars, less the ten percent commission.

The owner of the error, for a mere sixteen dollars, has established the going price of his stamps at eighty dollars, rather than the mere thirty dollars that the auctioneer originally felt it to be worth. The sixteen dollars has been a mighty sweet investment for the sheet's owner. A simple ruse, assuming that he owns one hundred stamps of this newly found error, has given him items on which the market has been established at eight thousand dollars, rather than three thousand.

In view of the rather dark picture painted here, let us get to the nitty gritty of auction buying and selling.

I have not made an attempt to count the number of auction houses in the world. If one were to include the tens of thousands of so-called "mail auctions," the number would be incredibly impressive. I prefer to regard an auction house as one that prints a regular catalog, which it mails to a substantial mailing list, which holds sales at regular intervals and which operates on the commission it earns from the sale of material belonging to other owners. There is nothing unethical in an auction house's putting its own material in a sale. If the house feels it can do a better job than another house in selling, there is no reason why it should not use its own services. The rub comes when it treats its own material differently from the material of others.

To sell a five shilling Sydney Harbour Bridge, belonging to another owner, at a bargain price, and hold back one's own because the price is not high enough is decidedly unethical.

Nor should one conclude that because an auction house meets the requirements above, it is automatically deserving of one's patronage, while a smaller "mail auction" house is not. Almost every top auction house today started as a small mail auction. Back in 1933, when I ran my first auction sale, every lot in the sale belonged to me. The admission should not be at all surprising. After all, what owner of desirable material is going to consign it to an untried, unproven auction house, without even an adequate mailing list? Before I graduated into operating an actual auction sale, with a hired auctioneer, and a crowd of active bidders. I conducted almost two dozen mail auctions, from which I garnered enough experience—and followers and owners—to venture into the big world of major auctioneering.

Mail auctions certainly have their place in philately. The costs of running a sale today are incredible. Just to print and mail a simple catalog can easily cost ten thousand dollars or more. To hire an auctioneer, rent a room and competent help can run another five thousand dollars or more. A sale properly advertised can add still more thousands of dollars. Obviously, any auction house selling, let us say, three thousand lots in a single sale, can easily run up costs of twenty thousand dollars before a single lot is sold. There has been no mention of license costs, insurance (a prohibitive item these days), travel, and even entertainment. Thus, if the cost of a sale averages seven dollars per lot, the lot itself must bring close to forty dollars just for the auction house to break even. And few auction houses can live very long on lots that earn only ten dollars or so.

Thus, mail auctions have their place, especially for those collectors whose philatelic needs are modest and who, much as they would like, find themselves unable to bid on the more expensive stamps found in the more important sales. But the one thought I do want to leave with readers is this: be it a formal auction sale, with bidders attending in person, or be it a mail auction, in which the only bidding is done by post, using these means to add to one's collection is a recommended way to obtain one's needs. It is unfair to condemn mail auctions as being dishonest or unhelpful, just as it is equally unfair to castigate formal auctions. Each form of buying has its advantages and each is as honest and reputable as the individual or individuals running it.

I feel that the most reprehensible act in conducting auction sales is the duplication of lots, at different prices. This is not done by reputable houses. It is easy to find out when this happens, and when one is certain of it, his course of action should be a simple one. He should confront the auctioneer with the deed, request that his name be removed from the mailing list and he should share his findings with all who will listen, provided of course, he is certain of his charges.

Duplicating lots at different prices is a shameful act. It takes advantage of the honest, generous bidder and rewards the cheapskate. Let us assume that Lot 28 is a British Penny Black, described as Fine. The highest bid on it is $80. There are also bids of $70, $60, and $50 dollars. Every bidder gets a lot. Perhaps the stamp at $50 may not be as fine as the original one, but although each of the unsuccessful bidders lost out on the lot, each finds that he has won one.

There is a splendid defense against this sort of thing: a list of realized prices. Almost every auction house that values its reputation provides a list of the prices at which every lot was sold. Duplicate prices are impossible for an auction house that prints the prices of the lots. Someone who may have paid seventy dollars for that Black Penny may wonder why it is mentioned as having sold for eighty dollars; the one who paid eighty dollars for it will be shocked if he runs across a friend who bought the same lot for sixty dollars. The list of prices at which each lot sold is a wonderful check on the auctioneer, and a steady inducement to refrain from doing any unethical act.

In all fairness I must say one thing. No one knows the value of stamps sold at auction in one year. It must surely be in the high hundreds of millions of dollars. Most of these stamps have not been seen by the prospective buyer; he bids on them simply by description. In no field of endeavor that I can think of is the possibility for fraud greater. In my own case, before retiring from the auction field in 1973, I sold many, many millions of dollars worth of stamps at auction over forty years.

I have not met as many as two percent of the buyers personally. Many lived in other countries. I did not know their ages, the color of their skin, their religions or even their marital status. It is a tribute to philatelists when I mention that in all those years, having trusted tens of thousands of collectors whom I had not, and never will meet, that my total losses on bad credit were well under ten thousand dollars.

What other business can boast of a similar accomplishment?

Many, many years ago, while at a political gathering intended to advance the campaign of a gentleman running for the United States Senate, I was introduced to another gentleman who was the "Commissioner of Licenses for the City of New York". I could not resist the opportunity to tell him that I had just sent his office a substantial check, to renew my Auctioneer's License.

"In what field?" he asked.

"Postage stamps," I replied.

His comment was pleasing to our ears: "We issue thousands of licenses for auctioneers, to Oriental rug salesmen, jewelry salesmen, firms that sell out bankrupt businesses and anything else one can think of. And five days a week we are holding hearings on complaints from the general public on these auctioneers. I cannot think of a single complaint since I have been in office against a stamp auctioneer. If every other auctioneer conducted himself as honestly as you guys do, there would be no need at all for my office."

8   It All Depends On What You Buy

Not too long ago some interesting comments by Robert Beall, a Portland, Oregon dealer, appeared in the always interesting publication of the Oregon Stamp Society, "The Album Page." I cannot guarantee his figures, and I doubt that Bob would care to either, but he stated that if one started buying mint United States stamps from the Post Office in 1960, right up to the year 1980, one would have spent $5,271.25.

This would encompass one pane of every stamp, ten complete booklets, and a strip of fifty of every coil—and the holding would resemble exactly the thousands of similar bundles of recent mint that one might sell for 90¢ or so on the dollar, if lucky. But had the collector visited his favorite dealer, and spent the same $5,271.25, today he would have an accumulation of desirable merchandise for which he could expect to get $35,591.

It is not important just how accurate the figures are. Even if the material purchased from a stamp dealer brought one-fifth of the total Beall states, he would be a heck of a lot better off than he would be had he given the money to Uncle Sam.

Many of us know all this. It is just absolutely impossible to tell it to the tens of thousands of people who flock to postal counters to buy quantities of panes of every new issue, thinking that this makes them philatelists. All they are doing is lending money to Uncle Sam, interest free money on which they have to lose.

33

9   A Shepherd in Wolf's Clothing

If you have never had the wonderful experience of sharing God's gift of love with as noble a creature as a dog, please, dear reader, turn the page and read no further. You just cannot understand.

Thousands of years ago, a wolf decided to leave his own kind, and being curious, walked close to man's abode. And the man, equally curious at coming close to quarters with an animal which had always been his enemy, welcomed him into his house.

Other wolves followed, giving up their own ways to adapt themselves to man's. They shared his home, his food and his ways. They even protected him against what had been their own kind.

Man learned to make use of his new friend's ability. He even changed the name by which he had been known. No longer was he a wolf. He was now a dog. No one knows where the name originated. Was it only a coincidence that man's new servant was a gift of that being whose name makes use of the same English letters?

Many thousands of years after man and dog formed a perfect relationship, a descendant of the primitive wolf came to live with us. And a true descendant he was, weighing almost one hundred pounds, and in appearance resembling a wolf... but only in appearance. Where his ancestors had been fierce, Alfie was gentle. Where his forefathers had attacked their two-legged enemies, Alfie regarded all of them as friends.

In his younger days, Alfie could play roughly. Once with a powerful sweep of his bushy tail, he knocked over and shattered a porcelain umbrella stand. He showed no remorse, for with all his intelligence, how was he to know that it was a priceless Meissen antique, and how could anyone scold him for such exuberance? Yet, when our infant grandchildren visited us, still unable to stand on their own feet, Alfie sized up the situation. He walked past them so lightly and gingerly, he might have walked on eggs.

Alfie's outer covering was varied in color, but we doubt if he ever was aware of that fact when he met descendants of other wolves. In his thirteen years, he set an example that man might emulate. He never sought to fight. He did not look at the color of other dogs; he approached all with head high, tail waving, in all friendliness and generally the friendliness was returned. Strange cats greeted Alfie in their typical unfriendly fashion, until they saw he meant them no harm. Minutes after their first meeting, they would invariably rub against his legs while he nuzzled them.

Alfie was a New Yorker. He was brought up in one of the coldest areas of New York State. When he moved to Florida, he did not understand the change in climate, but he adapted himself to it quickly. If his family were happy in Florida, he would be equally so.

Alfie became famous in postal circles in 1965. For some time, his master had daily been picking up the mail for a shut-in couple residing nearby, and Alfie daily made the trip, their mail in mouth. He learned to drop the letters on their porch and return to his master's side. A New York newspaper, the Daily News, heard of the dog in Shrub Oak that delivered the mail and their Sunday feature magazine wrote it up. During the 1970 postal strike in the East, a television network heard of his daily mail route and he became a national celebrity on the seven o'clock news when the network suggested that if the mail carriers would not work, dogs might be drafted.

The U.S. Information Service heard of Alfie and he was drafted by Uncle Sam as a propaganda tool. The Service "plants" stories and photos in publications all around the world, designed to show Americans, not as money-grubbing luxury-seeking capitalists, but as just plain folks, loving their dogs, among other things. We have stories on Alfie, together with photos of him faithfully delivering the mail, cut out of newspapers and magazines

Alfie reading his press notices.

35

published in Finland, Yugoslavia, Holland, France, Australia, the Philippines, and many other countries.

Alfie was elected mascot of the USS Alfred, a destroyer. He was allowed to become the seventh member of Scotland Yard's Police Dog patrol. He received a decoration from the Italian Post Office. In one week, Alfie received over five hundred letters from school children in Germany who had learned that he was honored on a postage stamp. And Alfie did not let the children down when they asked for his pawprint. Mrs. Herst resented the use of a stamp pad for the purpose (it left marks on the rugs) but Alfie never failed to extend his paw when the stamp pad was shown to him.

People used to ask if Alfie was a good watchdog. He was the best. Even if we did not hear the doorbell, Alfie always did. One loud bark was sufficient, just a single warning, perhaps repeated if we did not answer the bell promptly. But Alfie was a dog of few barks. He would always go to the door to see who it was. And whoever it was, to Alfie it was a good friend. He had no malice for anyone or anything.

Thirteen years is a ripe age for a German Shepherd. They say that a dog's life expectancy is one-seventh of a human, so Alfie would have been ninety-one. It is a ripe age. Were he a human, he might have lived through the Civil War, the 1893 Columbian Expositions, and he would have been well up in years when the Second World War came to an end.

At ninety-one, even the steps of a human grow faint. The hearing becomes impaired and the woes of accidents of years before worsen. (Alfie was run over by a truck in 1973, and he never really recovered normal use of his left hind leg.) In his last weeks, his venerable age showed more and more. Finally, he was mercifully put to sleep.

And Alfie, whose loyalty and faithfulness to those whom he loved was never qualified nor diluted, has found out that man can sometimes go back on his word. In his lifetime, he had been invited at death to be exhibited forever in the Smithsonian Institution's Hall of Communications, next to an equally famous postal dog who died almost half a century ago. But there is no longer a provision in the budget for an additional exhibit in Washington, so Alfie was cremated.

10   The Collector and the School Bus

The "Pat" nickname that I bear, in case anyone does not know, comes from a March 17th birthday. (St. Pat's Day, get it?) Many, many years ago, when you were still in swaddling clothes, I did a regular column for one of the philatelic weeklies entitled, "Here and There with Uncle Pat." I liked the sound of it, so how about one more time darting "Here and There with Uncle Pat"?

Many years ago, there was a stamp collector in Los Angeles named Harry Langlois. I knew from the stationery that Harry was one of a pair of brothers who manufactured school bus bodies. While in that city, I paid them a visit. The yellow bodies caught my eye.

"School buses ought to be readily identified," Harry told me. "Now they are every color under the sun and motorists cannot tell a school bus from any other. I would like to see every school bus in the country painted yellow. No telling how many kids' lives would be saved.

I think of that remark every time I stop for a school bus, and wonder if Harry is looking down on us and smiling each time kids get off that bus.

11   Nassau Street's Oddballs

The coziness of Nassau Street a half century ago, with perhaps a hundred or more dealers doing business within a strip only a thousand feet long, created characters that just cannot exist today. But for occasional feuding between one or two dealers, the philatelic oddballs who existed became apparent, and were known to all. Today, with stamp dealers scattered all over the countryside, there is no way for the Runyonesque characters to frequent a restricted area, as then happened.

I still recall Nosey, a bespectacled individual who acquired his nickname from stamp dealers because of what was really a nasal appendage. I first noticed Nosey about 1934, when he pressed his claim to a facial recognition against the window of a stamp shop, as if trying to get as close to the stamps as the glass would permit. Then one day Nosey entered the building at 116 Nassau Street, which at the time housed fifty or more dealers. He would stick his head in an office door and politely inquire, "Any errands?"

The subway then was a nickel, and we would often oblige by putting a blank sheet of paper in an envelope, or a couple of cheap stamps, address it to a dealer on the next block, or uptown, and Nosey would go on his way, fortified with a dime if it required a subway ride. Later in the day, he would return with the reply, which might be a sheet of paper or a couple of cheap stamps. His gratitude on being rewarded with a quarter's worth of stamps knew no bounds.

Nosey was a part of the philatelic world and he knew it. Even better, the dealers knew he could be trusted, and before long, he was carrying actual messages or delivering stamps. No one knew his name, nor where he lived. He was Nosey, and that was that. And one day Nosey was never seen again.

There also was Coca Cola. Few old-timers will recall his real name, but it was Morris Kohler. Coca Cola was a Russian and his thick accent had the flavor of the steppes in it. He was a guard at New York's main post office, passing mail trucks in and out of the cavern on 9th Avenue, into which they ventured to dispose of their mail. Cola had a gun when on duty, but he admitted he was so frightened of it he would never use it.

Postal salaries were pitiful in those days, but Cola had a second business that perhaps paid him better than did his post office job. The 1940s were the height of the matched plate number block fad. And what a fad it was, and what service he would give. If a new commemorative appeared on a Wednesday, by Thursday we had complete matched sets. "Around the Clock," they called it.

Of course, the secret was no secret to those of us who used Cola's courier service. He worked with someone on the inside, who would get right to work when the stamps came in, making up complete sets. Cola went off duty at four o'clock and he would head for Nassau Street. We were glad to pay him ten percent over face for the entire set; customers came in the next day, happy to pay us twenty or twenty-five percent over the face value.

Cola and his unidentified friend in the building (now known by its Zip code as 10001) had a good thing going. Of course, it was a cash business, with Cola's friend laying out the money for the stamps. But, since Cola's orders might amount to a thousand dollars or more at a time (plus subsequent re-orders), a single trip could easily return one hundred dollars, to be split evenly between them. One may be sure that his job with the post office did not pay fifty dollars per day.

Then there was the dealer who had a tiny hole-in-the-wall store in Hoboken, New Jersey, just across the river from Manhattan, and at the time a short ferry ride. His credit was not of the best. Let's call him Leonard J. Fish, which is not too far from his real name, which actually was another species of our finny friends.

Leonard one day came over to Nassau Street with a wad of cash, and made the rounds, paying off every one of his creditors. He was reluctant to state the cause of his good fortune, but he assured us that from then on, we need never worry about being paid promptly.

And so it was. It was a pleasure to deal with him, until one day we saw the headline in the newspaper:

BETTING RING SMASHED
STAMP STORE USED AS FRONT

It was indeed smashed. Leonard had sublet the back room to a nest of gamblers who installed phones and used it as their center of operations. He was fined a small sum and his credit rating on the street went back to zilch.

Enough years have passed that I can tell a true story that has never gone out of my typewriter, nor passed my lips. Bear in mind that in the 1940s and 1950s there were two stamp areas in New York: Nassau Street and the Grand Central area, around East 42nd Street. Most of the auctioneers were in the latter area. Just who made the arrangement we may never know, but illegal as it may have been it existed...and certain officials at Grand Central Annex (now 10017) must have known of it, or it could not have continued. No doubt everyone shared in the fees that changed hands...but truly, it was a service that made life much easier for stamp dealers.

Every day, about five in the afternoon, at the height of New York's rush hour (and no area of the city was more congested at that time than Grand Central), a post office truck would pull up at the curb of one of the several buildings housing stamp dealers. Fortified with this immunity from disturbance by New York's finest, the driver would visit the various dealers and take their first class mail, registered mail and parcel post to the truck. If one of the auctioneers was sending out auction catalogs, the dozen or so heavy sacks containing them were taken to the truck. Of course, the postal requirements, the listing of registered letters, and the statements for sending bulk mail were made out by the dealer and the driver would offer a receipt.

Illegal as the service may have been, there was no alternative. Just try taking a dozen sacks of catalogs in a taxi to a busy New York post office. Today, of course, there are services which perform the pickup and for the past quarter-century or more, the firm that prints most of New York's auction catalogs (Cosmos Press) takes care of all mailing details from their plant, away from midtown New York's congestion.

It is said that the stamp business today is quite different from what it was fifty years ago. There is little doubt that Nosey would find it impossible to continue his collecting today, and Cola would have trouble selling his matched plate blocks.

12   Robson Lowe's Greatest Find

Writing in The Philatelist *for June 1983, London's dean of auctioneers, Robson Lowe, mentioned an incident that shows us that tact, diplomacy and protocol play an important part in philatelic conversation in a country ruled by a monarch who has a stamp collection.*

Mr. Lowe was planning, with several others, for the London 1950 International Stamp Exhibition, for which H. M. King George VI was a Patron. The British Post Office needed a "knockout" exhibit, and Mr. Lowe happened to recall that in 1926, he had seen what was called a "Registration Book," containing what even then were exceptionally rare stamps.

Lowe and Sir John Wilson, Keeper of the King's Stamps, visited Sir Dudley Lumley, Controller General of the Post Office, with Robbie hoping to locate the book. Sir Dudley was not familiar with it, and suggested that Lowe's recollection was not correct. Sir John agreed, telling Lowe that it was evidently a daydream.

Lowe was quite sure that his recollection was correct, but did not press the matter further. However, when he returned to his office, there was a message for him to call Sir Dudley, which he did. "There is certainly such a book", Sir Dudley said, "but don't you realize that if I had brought it out in front of Sir John, he would have been obliged to take it for the Royal Collection?" Once the moment of danger had passed, the book was unbound, and some of its greatest rarities were shown at the Exhibition, without any comment from Sir John.

Lowe goes on to describe the exhibit as containing, among other things: "Cape of Good Hope 6d, slate purple, the Newfoundland 4d, orange, the New South Wales 8d laureated, the Nova Scotia 1851 1/-cold violet and the New Zealand 1855 1/-on blued paper. The Spanish stamps were exceptional, both for their brilliant condition and their rarity, and the 1851, 1852 and 1853 issues were complete but for the sixteen cuartos, which was only issued for domestic use. United States stamps were a mixed lot, with the 1857 issue complete, and it is of particular interest to note the high value of the State and Justice issues for the official department mail were registered at the General Post Office in London."

13   Diamonds are Forever? Never!

Being one of the more fortunate individuals who can make a living at home, I have a radio going the six or eight hours a day I spend at a typewriter. I know each commercial in the first two or three seconds. Some of them, in fact, give me the greatest touch of humor in the day.

One incredible advertisement is that of a jeweler who continues to make the rather amusing statement that diamonds are now bringing the highest prices in their history. True, the ad has not been changed in six years or so.

Those who moan about the low prices of many twentieth century stamps are in better shape than those who may have believed the diamond commercial while it was still young. In contrast, stamp "investors" have not suffered nearly as much.

Diamonds are not the only commodity that has turned sour. Whenever you are tempted to put money into an exotic investment scheme, be it a porcelain dish, a privately made pseudo-coin, or a stamp purporting to be from an uninhabited island, think about diamonds.

Investing in diamonds was all the rage several years ago. They were supposed to be the ultimate hedge against disaster. Now, every investment advisor can tell you stories about people who come to him for advice on how to sell the diamonds they bought while under the spell of a glib ad-writer.

The people who sold them the gems are either not interested or can no longer be found. And there is virtually no market for the stones—certainly not anywhere near the prices paid.

Several years too late to help anyone, the International Diamond Traders' Association came out with a statement condemning the sale of diamonds as an investment.

Your Zeppelins, souvenir sheets and recent plate blocks may not bring what you paid for them if they were bought at the top of the boom, but at least there are buyers for them... and while you owned them, admired them and proudly showed them, they were a great deal more enjoyable than a cold, uninspiring bit of jewelry.

14   A Letter From Australia

It may not be welcome news to residents of Savannah, Georgia, who claim to be among the earliest citizens of that lovely city, but in 1732, Lord Oglethorpe brought the first load of criminals to Georgia, which was considered to be the dumping ground for British prisoners. Ships continued to bring such human cargo to our shores, stopping only when our Declaration of Independence ended the practice. It was at that point, in the same decade with the Treaty of Paris ending the War, that Australia was substituted for this country.

This leads to my next experience. One of my columns in a Canadian newspaper brought interesting comments from its readers, mostly from our North American friends. It was a pleasant surprise recently to receive a letter from a reader in Figtree, N.S.W., Australia.

Geoff Telfer of that far off place was interested in a column which told how a number of Canadians involved in several of the various plots to divide Canada were unceremoniously, and without trial, shipped off to Australia where they could no longer be enemies of Canada while it was forging itself into a nation. Reader Telfer told me a little more about these Canadians, acting out of a sincere desire to do what they felt was good for Canada, who were subject to "Transportation" as the punishment was called.

Geoff told me that the Canadians were not alone in their plotting. Some Americans joined in the effort, and they shared the same fate as their Canadian friends, the only difference being that the Canadians were transported to New South Wales, while the Americans went to Tasmania.

Our Australian reader recommended a book that tells of these facts, written into a journal at the time by a French Canadian convict Francois Lepailleurs. A few years after it was published by the University of British Columbia, it was already out of print and greatly sought after. The English translation of the journal was edited by one F. Greenwood, and published under the title "Land of a Thousand Sorrows." Its scarcity is no doubt due to its very limited printing; it was not even sold in Australia.

Although Britain's trying to empty its jails by sending

miscreants to Australia is a well known story, there is very little literature to explain that not only did British subjects reach exile "down under", but also Canadians (and now, as we learn, Americans too). I have visited several libraries hoping to find more information, without success. Amazingly, in the most recent edition of the Encyclopedia Britannica, in dozens of pages on Australia there is not a single reference to the country's first immigrants from the New World.

Reader Telfer was kind enough to send me another book, which I shall enjoy reading. It is called "The Emerald Whaler," by William J. Laubenstein (the Companion Book Club, London. Just why the British, in their nonsensical obstinacy refuse to put on the title page either the date of copyright or the date of printing I shall never understand. This edition was printed in Australia, but just when is one of the mysteries of publishing.)

The book is an account of a transported Fenian who escaped from Australia, and was picked up at sea by an American whaler. The ex-prisoner, John Devoy, an Irish-American, conceived the bold plot of chartering a ship, taking it to Fremantle, Australia, where he had been imprisoned, and with a small crew invading the prison colony and taking on board the six Fenians who had been his companions in prison.

How they spirited the men from prison, how they got them to their ship, the Catalpa, and how the ship sailed for America under the noses of the prison guards who had not yet realized what had happened, is the story of the book. A British warship, the Georgette, did catch up with them at sea, but the Catalpa's master bluffed his way out of a confrontation. And on August 18, 1876, just weeks after the United States celebrated its first hundred years of freedom, a half dozen Fenians stepped ashore to enjoy their first days of freedom in many years.

Do many of us realize what a wonderful hobby we have? But for a single paragraph in a magazine article about Canadians being transported to Australia, I would never have known of this little bit of history, and thus readers would have been denied knowledge of it. And then a reader ten thousand miles away, on the other side of the world, contributes to the story, as he has in this article, and little by little the curtain is being torn away from a historical incident that seems to have been written out of the history books.

Canadian history is no less interesting than that of the United States. It started before U.S. history did; Quebec was already in existence when British colonists under Capt. John Smith founded Williamsburg. Do not be surprised if some day you may read more, if only I can find some historical references to the part that Canadians played in founding Australia.

And wouldn't it be exciting if some day someone were to turn up a letter from a Canadian Fenian who had been transported to Australia? It can happen. After all, there are letters known from Botany Bay, where most British convicts were settled.

15   The Stamp Collector's Anthem

Over the years, stamp dealers have tried just about every form of advertising except perhaps the Goodyear blimp (which blinks its lights at me several times a day as it passes over my house).

One of the oddest means of presenting a philatelic message was reserved for a London dealer named Palmer, who in the British stamp magazines coined the slogan in his advertising, "Palmer of the Strand." Palmer had a daughter who was gifted with a fine voice, and she used that asset professionally. She also frequented her father's office where, on occasion, she was known to break into a song.

Palmer wrote a song which he called "The Stamp Collector's Song." Just how large the printing was we may never know, but he put out a second printing, this time simply calling it, "Palmer of the Strand." In the first version, his daughter is alleged to be the author, while on the second his name appears. The year was 1880.

Years ago, when I had a collection of philatelic sheet music, Palmer's work was among them. Others were the well known "Postman's Gallop" and several with philatelic and postal titles. It has been years since I heard it played and sung. It was done at a stamp meeting in Columbia, South Carolina, to which I had been invited as a speaker.

Apparently Palmer did not think too well of some of his competition, for his song warned his customers to "beware of the scamp who deals in forged stamps." But if one buys his stamps from Palmer, "all his investments should prove safe and sound."

Here are all the verses of the song, with regret that the music score is not available:

> *Collectors there are of several sorts.*
> *The collector of taxes we all must respect.*
> *Some people will talk of collecting their thoughts*
> *And other poor souls have no thoughts to collect.*
> *The collector of China, of dishes and plates*
> *Is sometimes as cracked as the ware which elates*
> *But free from the freak of ill-fortune which damps*

46

Is the collector of postage stamps!
So here's to the praise of the best kind of craze
And the daily increase of our treasures.
For as long as it pays, let us follow the craze
The pleasure of kings and king of all pleasures.
With its fortune untold for the young and the old
It has charms for the judge and the rector
For the clerk on his stool and the youngster at school
Hurray for the stamp collector.
So here's to the praise of the best kind of craze
Hurray for the stamp collector.
The collector of stamps is paid for his pains
For all his investments should prove safe and sound
Whatever it is he may count on his gains
When he is in for a penny or in for a pound.
Like wine and cigars the stamps on your letter,
The older they get, the better.
So examine them well for sometimes they are sold
Like the lamp of Aladdin, new ones for old.
Beware of the scamp who deals in forged stamps
Who plunders in spite of legal measures
And beware of the reprint and forgery banned
And deal with Palmer of the Strand.
The law's vindicator, the famed exterminator
The champion of Parliamentary measures,
Is Palmer the protector, the inspector, the detector
The Minister in chief to the king of all pleasure.
With its fortune untold for the young and the old
It has charms for the judge and the rector
For the clerk on his stool and the youngster at school
Hurray for the stamp collector
So here's to praise of the best kind of craze.
Hurray for the stamp collector.

16   This Time The Ladies Won

There is a saying one hears in rural areas: you can take the boy out of the country, but you cannot take the country out of the boy. There is no philatelic parallel. You cannot take stamps out of the stamp dealer any more than you can take the stamp dealer out of the stamps.

I recall a party for philatelists and their wives given by the late Mrs. Robert Siegel at their home in White Plains, N.Y. So insistent were the wives that the evening conversations be on topics other than philately, that a large bowl was placed in the center of the room.

Each time that the conversation veered even remotely towards the philatelic, the offender was fined one dollar, the contents of the bowl to be divided among the wives at the end of the evening.

Surprisingly, the idea worked—for about ten minutes. And try as they did, the philatelists found it difficult to maintain the embargo. Slowly the bowl filled with dollar bills. And by 11 o'clock, we were making change, taking out four singles, and putting in a five.

Sorry, I do not recall the final score, but as the party broke up, the ladies were far ahead.

17   "By Pony Express"

It was April 3, 1860, one of the celebrated days in the history of philately. With cannons booming, and people in festive array, two riders, considered by most historians to be John Frey and Jas. Randall, started the saga of the Pony Express between St. Joseph, Missouri and San Francisco, California, one rider heading West, the other East. Thus started what is probably the most romantic period in the history of the carrying of the mails.

For the next 19 months the deeds of daring and valor that these and subsequent express riders undertook began the tradition of the Pony Express which still excites the world. Almost every hazard imaginable was encountered along the 1,966-mile route which operated through barren prairies, through Indian country, over mountains and desert. Land that previously had taken weeks and sometimes months to cross, now was traversed in from eight to 10 days.

Riders, undaunted by summer heat or winter snow and ice, operating with relays of horses, raced against time. They maintained schedules that, even today, would seem incredible. Neither the weather nor hostile Indians could stop these riders. They easily outran the Indian ponies in the open country, and traveled so fast that ambush attempts in the mountains were of little avail. The weather was taken as a matter of course. If a rider found no relief at the end of his seventy-five miles, he kept on going, and then doubled back. Several instances are recorded of a single horseman covering nearly 400 miles, stopping only to change mounts.

And all of this was done with the loss of only one mail in the more than 300 trips made.

In seven days and 17 hours, the news of Lincoln's election, carried by Pony riders, reached waiting Californians. By getting this information there ahead of any private agency, they are said to have saved the region west of the Rockies for the Union, and prevented it from becoming an independent state. Several conspiracies on foot there would have had it thus.

So much for the glamor of the hurrying hooves of the ponies and the heroism of the riders. There is another side to the story, a side far from glamorous wherein men's promises were unfulfilled and fortunes and reputations wrecked.

A "horse express" to California long had been talked of. Senator Gwin, of the state, first mentioned it to B. F. Ficklin, superintendent of Russell, Majors & Wadell, freighters of Leavenworth, Kansas, as early as 1854, while the two were traveling East together on horseback. The firm, however, was not at the time interested, as they were too busy with government contracts for carrying supplies to the Western Army Posts.

John Butterfield, who in 1858 began carrying mail under the first through overland mail contract, also talked of a "horse express," and in fact tried one trip with Buchanan's 1859 message to Congress. He made the 2,795 miles in some 12 days, and beat the best steamship time by four or five days.

Corner illustration from Butterfield envelope, circa 1860.

Butterfield's stagecoach route was known as the "Southern" and ran from St. Louis to Fort Smith, Arkansas, El Paso, Texas, Los Angeles, California, and thence to San Francisco, a route which reputedly had been chosen by Southern influence in Buchanan's Cabinet to try to bring California into the Southern fold.

The shorter "Central" route, as it was called, through Salt Lake City, Utah, reputedly was not approved for fear the

North would have an advantage in California.

In 1858, gold was discovered near Pike's Peak and a rush of immigration followed. Russell became enthusiastic over the possibility and suggested a stage line from Leavenworth to Denver, Colorado, but Majors, the monied man of the company, refused to join in the enterprise until the country was proven to be passable.

Russell went ahead on his own account and with a partner, Jones, established the Leavenworth City & Pike's Peak Express Company to run weekly stages between the two points. In three months the company's resources were exhausted and Majors, rather than see his old friend fail, took over the proposition.

The only way out seemed in expansion and toward that end the decrepit Holladay line of stages from "St. Jo" to Salt Lake was taken over, and the two lines merged into a new company, the Central Overland California and the Pike's Peak Express.

In the meantime the contractor for the line between Salt Lake and Placerville, California was said to be about to default, and on representations from Russell, the Postmaster General transferred that contract to the new company.

Thus, in a few short months the shorter Central route, backed by adequate capital, loomed as a serious competitor of the Southern, a situation which, it seemed, pleased neither the Butterfield interests nor the reputed ruling powers in Washington.

At that time, the government owed Russell, Waddell & Majors large sums on past freighting contracts which could not be paid on account of the condition of the Treasury. And J. H. Floyd, Secretary of War, entered into the unauthorized practice of issuing acceptances for services performed and to be performed to transfer large quantities of war supplies to the Southwestern Army Posts. The banks refused to honor these acceptances, and so, to allow the contracts to continue, Floyd reputedly caused certain government bonds to be given to Russell as security, the bonds to be returned when the acceptances were paid.

Russell also busied himself about the mail contracts of the

Central Overland, which were to expire in a little over a year. Senator Gwin offered to help and suggested nothing was needed more than a thorough demonstration that there was nothing in the stock argument that the Central route was impassable in winter, and that the best way to show this was by a "horse express," which would cover the distance in 10 days.

An advertisement of this kind could not do otherwise than bring a renewal of the contracts on the basis of a profit rather than the losing proposition they then were. Gwin also promised that he would secure a subsidy to cover the cost of its installation and upkeep once the "horse express" was a going reality.

Whether Russell really believed Gwin could carry out his agreement or was simply carried away by enthusiasm never will be known, but at any rate, Russell convinced the skeptical Majors that the word of the firm had been pledged and so nothing remained but to go on with the Pony Express, as it now was called.

Consequently (and at enormous expense), they built stations every 10 or 12 miles from "St. Jo" to Placerville, secured the necessary horses, equipment, and men, and announced April 3, 1860, as the starting date.

The Pony Express was a good advertising promotion. The whole country talked about it, and had future contracts depended on its popularity there would have been no question of the result. But like many another road show, it did not pay.

Gwin fell down on the subsidy. As the months went on, the government payments on the freight contracts got slower and slower. Russell, Majors & Waddell began to need money. The initials of the Central Overland California and Pikes Peak Express Company (C. O. C. & P. P.) was said by the press of the day to stand for "Clean Out of Cash and Poor Pay."

1861 C.O.C. & P.P. handstamp

To keep going, the Company borrowed large sums from Ben Holladay, another freight contractor, and possibly from Wells Fargo & Company, which had secured control of the Southern Overland.

To make matters worse, in December 1860, a scandal broke in Washington. Floyd's use of the acceptances and bonds caused Floyd, Russell and a clerk to be indicted for conspiracy to defraud the government. Floyd and the clerk fled South. Russell insisted on his innocence, but he evidently made good the amount of the bonds, for the indictment was never brought to trial, nor has any report of the Congressional investigation ever been found. Of course, very soon after this, the nation was involved in civil war.

The final blow, which completely destroyed this once great company, came when the lame duck Congress of 1861, just before adjournment on March 2, altered the contract with the Overland Mail Company, which had operated over the Southern route. Reportedly to prevent its falling into the hands of the Confederate States, this route was moved north to the Central route, and the C. O. C. & P. P.'s hopes of obtaining the Central route contract were extinguished.

With this, Holladay foreclosed on Russell, Majors & Waddell. The Overland Mail Company, which now controlled the route, signed contracts by which with the C. O. C. & P. P. Express Co. would operate the Pony route east of Salt Lake City, and Wells, Fargo & Company would run a "fast express" west of Salt Lake City. It was under this arrangement that the famed Wells, Fargo & Company became the agents for the handling of the mail west of Salt Lake City, and subsequently issued their Pony Express stamps.

1861 usage of the $2 Red Wells, Fargo stamp (Scott 143L1)

18   When Worlds Collide, Philatelists Gain

The world of art, just as is true in the world of stamps, is a peculiar one. Works of art by members of the Royal Academy generally bring substantial sums, when offered for sale by the prominent auctioneers of London and New York. But for some reason, if the work of art is philatelic, that is not true. In fact, if it is a philatelic item, its value is but a few dollars.

William Etty (1787-1849) was a painter who studied at the Royal Academy School, which was then in Somerset House in London. His first exhibit was in 1811, but not until his famous painting, "Cleopatra," was shown in 1821 was he invited to become part of the Academy. His "Joan of Arc" soon after sold for two thousand five hundred pounds, then about twelve thousand dollars, an incredible price for a living artist. His paintings can be found today in London's National Gallery and in the South Kensington Museum.

Two years before his death, in 1847, he was in Brighton, a seacoast resort south of London, and he had occasion to write to Richard Haines, of 51 New Bond St., London. Reference to directories of the time show that Haines was a poultry dealer at that address. (If one needed evidence that neighborhoods change in London as elsewhere, here it is. That address today is one of the finest commercial addresses in the world.)

Perhaps the artist had time on his hands, there being little in Brighton to do in midsummer but watch the clouds pass by. We shall never know, but Etty, not content with addressing the cover to his poultry dealer, decided to make it a work of art. With delicate strokes, he painted the figures of four young ladies on the envelope, in varying states of dress and undress. He posted the letter in Brighton on July 24, 1847; it was delivered to London, as shown by the backstamps, later that day. (One could hardly expect that sort of service today.)

What would one expect to pay for an original miniature painting done by a member of the Royal Academy almost a century and a half ago?

Surprise! Not very much. The cover was included with several other hand-illustrated covers, in a London stamp auction. The selling price was considerably less than one hundred dollars.

And lest one think that the auction describer may have been unaware of Etty's reputation, I hasten to add that on the page on which the former owner had mounted the cover, Etty's entire life history was told...and it was from that accounting, clipped from a page listing members of the Royal Academy, that I obtained the facts as stated earlier in this article.

It is indeed difficult to understand why members of the world of art choose to ignore the philatelic aspects of the field in which they are engaged. It was much the same in the field of autographs until this generation. Autographs and manuscripts have always fascinated me, and when I started being a devout philatelist, a half century ago, a George Washington letter might bring one hundred dollars, but a franked cover less than one fifth of that. A signed Lincoln document could be purchased for one hundred fifty dollars, while a franked cover could be found for thirty-five dollars. Even today, it is philatelists' awareness of their desirability, and not that of autograph and manuscript collectors, that has raised the price of presidential franks.

Finally, lest you think philately is perfect, consider this: A stamp, of which but a single example exists (such as Poonch No. 1A), sold for $850 in a London auction a few years ago. Others, such as the famed twenty-four cent inverted air mail, of which at least ninety-four are currently known to exist, has sold for more than one hundred eighty thousand dollars. The world of stamps, just like the world of art, can be peculiar.

19   Better Check Your McReas and Dees

It was October 1937. My wife and I were driving to the American Philatelic Society convention in New Orleans, and we arrived early in the evening in the small town of West Point, Georgia. Motels were not yet known, and most travelers by car spent the night in tourist houses, usually for a dollar per person. Hotels were much more expensive.

We found a place, unloaded the car, and started out looking for a restaurant. We were about to finish our meals when a couple of dozen students rushed in, presented snips of paper, theater programs and autograph books at us. "Your autograph, please" they said.

We did not understand the request. One young man said "We know who you are. We were told that you and your wife had left the hotel and had gone out for dinner. We saw your car with New York plates on it, so we knew you were here."

I asked whom we were supposed to be. Several answered at once. "Joel McCrea and Francis Dee". We laughed and denied it. "What makes you think so?" we asked. "We know movie people try to hide who they are. All we want, Mr. McCrea, are your autographs."

In vain did my wife and I try to tell them we were not the couple they thought we were. My wife was attractive enough to be taken for Frances Dee, but by no stretch of the imagination might I pass for Joel McCrea. But there was no convincing the crowd, which grew larger by the moment.

There had been a play presented at the West Point High School that night, and it had just ended. The drama coach mentioned to the cast that a famous movie couple was spending the night in West Point at the hotel. The cast mentioned it to friends. Some of those who were in the play were carrying printed programs of the show.

"Please sign, please sign, please sign" the crowd continued. "I want it for my sick brother. My mother will scold me if I don't get it. We know who you are. Please. Please. Please."

How do you convince people under those circumstances that you are not famous? Finally I told them that I would sign, but only if they would let me sign my real name. I signed a couple of programs on that basis. They were not satisfied. "Don't kid us. We know who you are. Please. Please. Please."

There was no satisfying them. The proprietor came over and told us that he was going to have to ask the kids to leave. They were disrupting the other diners. He begged us to give the kids autographs. It was time to close up and he would have to pay his help overtime.

We had no choice. We obliged. We finished our meal, and walked to the cashier to pay the bill.

"I wouldn't think of charging you, Mr. McCrea," the proprietor said. "Just do me one favor. Will you each sign your names to the bill, and I will put it on the wall?"

It has been a half century. I have never been back to West Point, Georgia, and I often wonder if it is still on the wall. But for a good many years after the incident, I think that the citizens of that Georgia town will talk of the night Mr. & Mrs. Joel McCrea spent a night in their town.

I often get catalogs of dealers who sell autographs of famous people, including movie stars. I note that Joel McCrea and Frances Dee are usually priced at $5 or $10 each. Perhaps they are worth it. But if you ever see one on a restaurant bill, don't buy it. It probably is a fake.

And does my conscience hurt me? It does now when I look back on that evening, but one thing is certain. A lot of kids, and a few adults, went to bed that night happier than they otherwise might have been.

20   Pollution in New York, 1783 Style

It is not only in recent years that prospective visitors to New York City were warned against the hazards of travel in the metropolis. A visit to New York even in 1783 might also be hazardous to one's health.

New York City was still occupied by the British Army in April 1783 when Judge Timothy Edwards, of Stockbridge, Massachusetts (1783-1813) wrote his good friend, Aaron Burr, with some advice about Burr's plans to visit New York. Judge Edwards wrote Burr as follows:

Stockbridge   April 8 1783

Dear Burr—

I am just returned from New York. It is a sad place into which to carry a family at present—I am much mistaken if pollution both natural and moral should not prevail there very much this summer—

I pray you to be deliberate in going there. It will be two if not four months before the British will leave it.

Your pork and gammons are engaged but not yet at the landing—The last are not full cured. Do not send them until I see you—I have been from home a month, my family have either neglected your horse or he is unwell. I am not satisfied which is the case—Do not send for him at present if you can do without him.

The Honble. John Worthington Esq. must be a referee in the stead of Mr. Otis. Col. Wadsworth refuses. We are all well—Mrs. Edwards joins us, complt. to Mrs. Burr—with much affection, Adieu.

Timy. Edwards

21 The Famed Brooklyn Sheriff's Stamp Sale

It really does not take very much to spark a long forgotten memory in what passes for a brain in my white-topped head. A couple of words, a short article, or even a headline: "Bridge Ceremony to Take Place in Brooklyn Borough Hall" That did it.

The ceremony referred to the stamp just issued for the centenary of the Brooklyn Bridge, at the time called "the eighth wonder of the world."

Brooklyn Borough Hall! I wonder how many there are who remember an impromptu auction of stamps that took place there about 1936.

The Sheriff of Kings County, which is the county name for the Borough of Brooklyn, part of New York City since 1898 (See Scott #C38), occasionally would sell stamp collections that for one reason or another came into his hands.

Occasionally the police would turn up some stamps. Once a collection was found on the subway, and sold at auction. And occasionally stamps might be found in an abandoned house that the city took for taxes. Do not forget economic conditions in the 1930s.

It was the sale in a basement room at Brooklyn's Borough Hall that I remember well. Penny postal cards were sent to every dealer in the telephone classified directory, with time and place noted, and the rather incredible statement that inspection of the lots would not be permitted.

Some of us phoned the telephone number on the card, asking why inspection was not permitted. "Last time we had inspection, we had such a crowd of people they could not possibly be watched," we were told. "By the time the sale started, half of it seemed to have disappeared."

Prospective bidders were told that they could go to Borough Hall and get a mimeographed list of the stamps to be sold. About all it revealed was the color of the album. Each album was sealed tightly with adhesive tape! Scotch tape was some years in the future.

Inspection of the material to be sold was a fruitless task.

One could, of course, buy by weight, on the theory that a two pound album was worth twice the price of a one pounder, but what was the one pounder worth?

Came the afternoon of the sale and about one hundred dealers showed up, most of us known to one another. We recognized one chap helping with the sale, who told us: "I have a list with the value of every lot. I work in Probate, and I spent an afternoon valuing them. The list will cost you ten bucks."

He sold perhaps two dozen lists. Those who bought compared the valuation with the heftiness of the lot. Vainly they sought some formula they might use. Reference to the city-supplied list offered no help. "One green album," it read, or "six large envelopes." There was no indication of contents, on either list. The lot might contain U.S. or foreign, mint or used, bulk stamps or covers.

Common sense told those attending that what the sale would come down to would be finding out who would be the biggest gambler in exceeding the estimates on the ten dollar list. What crossed my mind was the possibility that if one chap had been able to look at the stamps, perhaps another one had—and the possibility that the chap selling the list might intentionally price low the better lots that he wanted to buy, and price high those he would not want.

It turned out that both of these possibilities were correct. Most of Nassau Street went home empty-handed, or with material for which they had grossly overpaid. The bulk of the lots went to two individuals. One of them was the chap who had sold the list for ten dollars.

22   The Postal History of Christmas

Philately can indeed be made to pay, if one keeps his eyes open, and recognizes value when it passes by. A reader in Alameda, California wrote to tell us of the good buy he made at a flea market in Alameda. He found an old postcard album, mostly of views of England and France. While thumbing through, he noticed a card picturing Manchester, with a very common Edward VII stamp, but with an unusual postmark, showing a large X and a series of straight horizontal lines. He sent me a copy of it and he received good news.

In the first decade of this century, when Christmas greetings were beginning to flood the postmen, one could post his cards ahead of time in Britain and they would be held until the proper time; others had an oval, with the words, "Posted in Advance for Delivery on Christmas Day." Some used the somewhat offensive abbreviation "XMAS." There are several types known. The earliest use of the "advance" postmark that I recall is 1902, and the latest, 1909, although there well may be earlier and later ones.

The California collector had paid ten dollars for the entire album; the Manchester Christmas marking brought seventy-five dollars when sent to a British auction sale, along with other philatelic material of British significance. Then he sold the remainder of the album to an Oakland antique store for twelve dollars and fifty cents. Aside from perhaps coin collecting, how many other hobbies are there that can bring the pleasure philately does, and still more than pay their own way?

And while on the subject of Christmas, can any reader make a guess as to the date of the earliest Christmas greeting? There are all sorts of statements, all wrong, unless one reports 1840 as the year.

The printers were Messrs. Fores, then located 41, Piccadilly in London's West End. In May, 1840, Rowland Hill came up with two ideas to make the prepayment of postage on letters possible. One was an adhesive stamp, the other an envelope and lettersheet. The stamp was popular; the postal stationery less so.

Various printers took advantage of the dislike for the

61

envelope and lettersheet by caricaturing it. Fores produced a number of different designs. Their earlier ones merely poked fun at the Mulready design, but then, realizing that they were onto a good thing, they began to produce envelopes with themes. Fores No. 1 was their "Courting Envelope," for dashing swains to use when writing to their loves; No. 2 was for musicians, No. 3 for dancers, No. 4 for fox hunters, others were for shooters, civic employees (picturing a well fed politician, spirits in hand, astride a giant turtle), etc.

Then came No. 10, Fores' Christmas envelope, which appeared in time for the 1840 holiday season. It shows all the trappings familiar at Christmas to the average Briton: a plum pudding, a Punch and Judy show on the march, carolers, angels with garlands and a Christmas cake.

The custom of sending greetings at Christmas is thus tied up with our first postage stamp, the gift of Sir Rowland Hill to the world, more than a century and a half ago.

Coming back to the present time, I hope that collectors will recall this admonition: True, green and red are the traditional Christmas colors, but philatelists should remember to save them for everything but the envelope in which their holiday greetings are mailed.

There is no way of knowing how many commemoratives are ruined each Christmas by having been soaked along with colored envelope paper that runs when wet. The courtesy of a commemorative on the envelope is appreciated, but the thought loses its significance when not only that stamp, but others soaked in the same batch are irreparably ruined by the envelope dyes.

23   The Dealer is Mentally Ill, and Excused

The first stamp dealer we have record of was William P. Brown. Handicapped with one arm, New York's Postmaster let him beg for stamps at the Nassau Street Post Office as people came to pick up their mail. (The only delivery to home or office was performed by the local post companies for an extra fee.)

Brown sold his stamps by pinning them to a board at the edge of City Hall park. He did this for some years before he opened an office in one of the rabbit warrens that passed for offices in New York. By the 1880s, Brown and dozens of others were located in offices along Nassau Street, and philately had arrived as a premier hobby.

Brown was called as a witness once, in a non-philatelic case, and being an atheist he refused to take an oath on a Bible. It was in 1881, and he was called upon to testify in New York's Court of Common Pleas, with Judge Van Hoesen presiding.

The judge told Brown that unless he took the oath he would be sentenced to 30 days in jail. Brought before the bench, Brown's lawyer was informed by the Judge, "It has been suggested that the man is not sane. I will make some inquiries and if I find that he is of sound mind, I will certainly enforce the law. His offense is criminal contempt."

Brown served five days in jail and was fined $25.00. His lawyer's attempt to have the sentence mitigated again brought him before the judge. For the first time, Brown's occupation as a dealer in stamps for collectors was brought to the judge's attention.

The judge remarked: "Had the court known that, we would have had no difficulty at all in establishing that anyone who dealt in old postage stamps must certainly be insane, and on that score he would have been ineligible to have served as a witness."

24 The Law of Diminishing FDC Returns

Many times in stamp magazines, I've tried to put some common sense into the heads of those misguided speculators who are still spending their money with Uncle Sam for quantities of current plate number blocks or complete panes of commemoratives. But the vast American public does not subscribe to stamp magazines, and it is they who sink their hard earned money into stamps and/or covers that will never bring a price near what was paid for them.

We cannot blame Uncle Sam. He is issuing fifty or more different stamps a year because there are so many people not content with buying one block, or one plate number block. With a bomber costing hundreds of millions of dollars, or more, the money from stamp collectors would not even buy much more than the wings, but it all helps.

Sixty years ago, quantities of commemoratives issued were as few as fifteen million; now they can run into the hundreds of millions. And sixty years ago, few people bought plate blocks or panes at the post office; today hundreds of thousands do. There is no way to overrule the law of diminishing returns.

As with current mint plate blocks, the collector of first day covers must play by the rules if he wishes to find his collection in demand when he desires to dispose of it.

One facet of collecting that did not exist three-quarters of a century ago was the collecting of stamps used on cover on the day of issue. This is not to say that first day covers of our early stamps do not exist; there are quite a few known of the three cent 1851 (Scott #10, photo), a fact not too surprising, since on July 1, 1851, the day that stamp came into use, tens of thousands must have been used. In my half century or more of professional philatelic activity, I have found three, two of them bringing great pleasure to the owners, who did not realize what they had. (Scott prices one at $7,500 today. Why not start looking yourself?)

There is very little demand for ordinary plain envelopes used on first day covers since 1923. Of course, on the rare early issues, this does not hold, for as explained, the collecting of first day covers was an activity practiced by only a handful of collectors. But in the 1920s, a touch of interest was added to first day covers by the presence of what is called a cachet. A cachet simply is printing, or a picture, at the left of the envelope, telling something about the stamp or the circumstances of its issue. This may be printed. It may be hand-painted in color. (Once frowned upon, these hand-drawn covers are becoming increasingly popular.) The cachet may be engraved; today most of them are. In the 1920s and into the 1930s, cachets were even rubber stamped, although these are not too popular among collectors.

ArtCraft engraved cachet for the Savings Bonds stamp, issued
April 30, 1991, but with a cancellation error date of January 22.

Collectors of FDCs (as they most often are called) may find it difficult to explain why unaddressed covers are in much greater demand than those that actually went through the mail. Although the fact defies logic, it must be reckoned with.

Book collectors are no less victims of a similar inexplicable syndrome. An antique book with the pages uncut, indicating that it has never been read, will always be worth more than one with the pages cut, despite the fact that the book was originally published to be read.

The demand for unaddressed covers can be traced to one person, Frederick Rice of Virginia. Fred ran one of the early first day cover services. One could send him a deposit, and be assured of a new cover of every new stamp. Since there were times that the Post Office did not give advance notice, collectors of FDCs found that they missed certain issues, and had to visit dealers, and accept a different envelope (or a different cachet).

Some collectors sought uniformity in their covers, and asked Fred to send them inside another cover, so that in their own handwriting, they might add their name, thus giving a tone of similarity to the collection. Fred obliged, and he charged two prices for his covers, those addressed which came under their own power through the mail, and the unaddressed, which came in another envelope. Thus was created the unaddressed FDC.

Today almost every first day cover service delivers unaddressed covers to its customers. And to add a note of absurdity to FDC collecting, the postmark on the cover need not bear any relation to the place where it was postmarked. In fact, Uncle Sam permits some large FDC distributors to do their own postmarking, on their own premises, perhaps thousands of miles from the office designated as the one for FDC's. Ostensibly, this system can lead to abuses. Although a government official is supposed to be on hand to prevent them, some abuses have occurred.

25   1814, A Year In Review

Newspapers, as we know them today, began in the late 1600s. To obtain a copy, one simply walked to the place of publication and bought it. It was not long before youngsters took on the job, doing it simply for the reward they would receive on delivering it. So traditional is the occupation that even today, our child labor laws and our minimum wage laws specifically exclude newscarriers.

If you are among those who remember your friendly, faithful newscarrier at Christmas time, and we hope you are, you are helping to carry out a tradition that goes back to newspaper's earliest days. Come Christmas, the newscarrier would traditionally receive an especially large gift, hopefully large enough to encourage him to continue his labors through another year. To make certain that they would not be forgotten, some newscarriers in the second decade of the last century printed Christmas greetings, which they delivered with their papers a few days before. Sometimes they were in rhyme, and sometimes summarized the news of the previous year, no doubt as a reminder of their services.

While we were in London some years ago, we visited the British Museum to examine their collections of newscarriers' addresses. Their earliest was from Christmas, 1816, something we were happy to learn, for shortly before our visit we had acquired one from two years earlier. It was our pleasure subsequently to present them with it.

Our 1814 version was in the form of a poem, but whether written by the newsboy himself (a doubtful assumption) or gleaned elsewhere (as is likely) we cannot say.

In 1814, Britain was fighting for its life on battlefronts all over the world—in India, in the Caribbean, in Spain, in the Near East—and in America, the latter conflict known to us as the war of 1812. But it was merely a small segment of what was actually a world war on a scale that history had never known before.

Napoleon was, of course, Britain's primary enemy, but local issues on battlefields thousands of miles apart often took on a different significance. In view of Britain's traditional friendship with the United States, today we smile at John Bull's calling this country its "treach'rous foe" and its seeking "Victory from the Yankee strand," but in the light of the world's unsettled condition at that time, we were no doubt calling Britain even worse.

"The Newscarrier's Address," dated Christmas, 1814, is still a splendid accounting of what today's newspaper brings its readers each day:

"At Christmas time, each cheerful heart
Delights it bounty to impart
To those who, by some faithful serving
Acquire the title of 'deserving'.
This Title, then, pray not refuse
To HIM who brings the Weekly News
Of Battles lost, of Battles won
The glorious race our Heroes run,
On ocean's wave, or tented field,
How well they've fought—how scorn'd to yield.
Depicted in my Weekly page,
You've seen the Tyrant in his rage,
With murd'rous bands the world oppress,—
You've also seen the world's redress.
Britain's brave sons first stemm'd the tide
Led on by Wellington—our pride!
The sparks he kindled spread around
Lo! Tyranny is beaten down,
The Monster to his Exile goes,
'The jest of Fools', the scorn of foes.
But War alone claims not my care,
I bring you Fashions for the Fair,
The jeu d'esprit—the well-told story
And Plaintive Songs of Love—or Glory.
In short, I bring, in Prose or Rhyme,
'The form and pressure of the time'
Thus having given you various treats
(A Glorious Peace, and Royal Fetes)
A Christmas Box, pray not refuse
To your obedient Carrier Of The News"

26   My $64,000 Question

When I lived in New York, I was an infrequent guest on some of the panel quiz shows. I had been placed in the Goodson-Todman computer as an expert on trivia; that is the company that put the shows together. And if you want to know if I won any money, the answer is yes, although the prizes were much more modest in those days than they became later, during the quiz show craze.

Each panel decided before the show whether one could be selfish and keep all of one's winnings or divide them among the panel; the check was never a large one, and even then went to charity. Now, as then, I would say that the stamp collector who really knows his stamps will outperform the ordinary citizen in games such as Trivial Pursuit, unless of course the questions concern movie stars, or those with diseased tonsils who emit sounds befitting a hog-calling contest, and are called singers.

Trivia comes naturally. Take the waterbed, for example. Who invented it? I will wager there are not two people in this country who can answer that question, if there are indeed two. I know there is one: me. The waterbed is the invention of one Dr. J. K. Abbott. His idea was simple: a waterproof sack, with an outer inner cell (figure that one out!) of air, and a mattress consisting principally of water. And darned if the illustration did not look exactly like the waterbed of today.

Now that it would cost several hundred dollars for game show producers to bring me to a New York studio from Florida, it is not likely that I am still in their computer. But I can dream, can't I?

...The prize is $64,000. The armed guards stand at attention. (To assure that the program is honest, they use vice presidents—which should make me suspicious right away.)

Comes the question: Who invented the waterbed, what was it called, and when was it publicly advertised? And comes the answer: Dr. J. K. Abbott, the Hydrostatic mattress, in 1840.

And then I wake up, with the sound of water dripping. Yes, it is raining; Good thing. I thought for a moment my hydrostatic mattress was leaking.

27 The Kansas-Nebraskas

It is surprising how many collectors attempt to collect intelligently without a catalogue. It is true that each year new catalogues cost more, since each year there is more to them, but at the very reasonable price at which an older catalogue can be purchased, such economy hardly is justified.

Newer collectors, especially those not possessed of a catalogue, sometimes are puzzled by stamps that bear an overprint reading "Kans." or "Nebr." The "Kansas and Nebraska" issues of 1929 form a very interesting chapter in collecting. Many collectors, when they first see them, feel that they are precancels. This belief, incorrect though it may be, has historical precedent.

When the issues originally appeared, many Post Offices outside of those two states refused to accept them, not knowing their origin. In those days, some of the large mail-order houses accepted postage remittances for small or odd sums. But when these businesses attempted to use some of the stamps on their own mail, their letters occasionally were returned, or marked "Postage Due."

It was the original idea to overprint all regular issues up to the 10-cent values in each of the 48 states; the stamps to be put on sale in that form in the smaller Post Offices, which were, of course, the ones most likely to be robbed, because of insufficient security.

The plan was that a robbery of an office in Kansas, for example, would make the stamps suspect if increased numbers suddenly appeared on mail from Oklahoma, and if offered for sale in the state where the robbery had taken place, the stamps would be even more suspect.

Ample philatelic and general notice was given. The stamps consisted of 11 values, from the half-cent to the 10-cent. May 1, 1929, saw the first day of sale. Because of the novelty of the issue, philatelic sales were considerable. The sets also were placed on sale at the Philatelic Agency in Washington the same day.

First Day Cover collecting was even then a popular hobby, and quite a number of sets were placed on covers to receive the first day cancel. As always happens, a few were used earlier, so that pre-first day covers are known.

The scheme was abandoned a few months after it was instituted, and collectors lost interest in it when it was decided not to extend the idea to all other states in the Union.

For a few years the stamps were easily available at slight premiums over face value, despite the fact it generally was known that three stamps in the two sets, the 6, 7, and 10-cent Nebraska each were printed in a quantity of much less than a million. In fact, slightly more than a half million of the 10-cent were issued.

The fact that these were printed on the rotary press, which, during that period usually meant very poor centering, no doubt had a great deal to do with the disfavor the issue met. Commemoratives were extremely popular at the time, and these were not commemoratives.

However, albums provided spaces for them, and with the tremendous depression boom that philately enjoyed, collectors suddenly sought the Kansas-Nebraska issues out, and found the market bare. A half million sets available, and much of them used up and destroyed by the non-philatelic public, made an ugly duckling seem like a beautiful swan.

Fakers rushed to fill the gap. The stamps even could be imitated with a typewriter. We still occasionally see collections with fakes of these issues that had been produced on the typewriter. They are easily spotted.

When Uncle Sam printed these stamps, they were overprinted before they were gummed. Thus, when examined on the back, you cannot see a raised outline of the letters in the gum. Any overprint placed on the stamp after gumming would show the letters raised in the gum. The period that follows the four letters would especially stand out.

Faking the used is a much easier job, as after adding the letters, the stamp can be ironed or subjected to such pressure that the raised letters and/or period can be flattened. The writer would estimate that more than half of the used sets of Kansas and Nebraska in collections today are counterfeit.

A goodly number of mint sets in collections are suspect as well, though not to the same degree. There are a number of other tests available for mint stamps that make it not too difficult for any philatelist worthy of the name to test the unused specimens.

For one thing, since the Bureau of Engraving and Printing made only the one printing of the Kansas-Nebraska stamps, color shades on the basic stamp do not exist. For example, we often see in collections fakes of the 8¢ stamps that were made on shades which themselves did not appear until the early 1930s, long after the Kansas-Nebraska issue had been laid to rest.

There are distinctive late printings of some values which are especially recognizable, such as the 4-cent, 5-cent, 6-cent, 7-cent and 8-cent. In many sets, the low values, especially the 1-cent, 1 1/2-cent, and 2-cent are certain to be genuine. Even today, they are so cheap it hardly pays to counterfeit them, and a mixed set easily allays suspicion.

Plate number blocks on these stamps are today exceedingly rare. They bring $500 and up per set, depending on the centering. In fact, a well-centered set of these blocks, were it to come up at auction today, would undoubtedly bring in excess of catalogue.

Fakes are less likely to appear on plate number blocks than on the stamps themselves, but we have seen them. The difficulty with faking plate blocks is the difficulty of finding the "raw material."

Since the Bureau kept a record of all of the plate numbers used on this series, to fake a set means finding 22 different plate number blocks, each with the proper number recorded as having been used. This is a job which will discourage the average faker, who is generally too lazy to do things right.

As a rule, he does not need to extend himself. There always seem to be collectors who do not take the trouble to learn about their stamps, despite the ease with which the proper literature can be obtained. It is our experience that most collectors are victimized through lack of knowledge.

28   Crooked Advertising on Both Sides of the Atlantic

There are times when we can learn from what is done in other countries, just as more often, other countries can learn from us. It is unfortunate that there is nothing in this country similar to the Advertising Standards Authority.

Britain has such an Advertising Standards Authority. It is a totally unofficial board, which investigates complaints of improper advertising. The Authority is supported by a voluntary assessment on the advertising income of Britain's magazines, including stamp magazines.

If on investigation the complaint of a reader is found to be valid, the Authority has the right to deny the advertiser the right to advertise in British magazines for a period of time, which might be as long as six months.

One of Britain's top firms once was adjudged guilty of a violation of the code. It had offered a "limited edition of a Commonwealth Day collection" that was represented to be a "unique and historic investment opportunity."

Of course the collection was by no means unique. Had it been, the firm would not have been able to offer more than one. (Actually, "only" 20,000 of the special "unique" collection were to be sold.) Additionally, the complainant alleged that the face value of the stamps was £60, and the price at which it was advertised was £150, thus making it in all likelihood a mighty poor investment.

In defense, the firm stated that the collection included a number of items not available elsewhere, thus making the price not as excessive as one might think. Some of these additional features included a "certificate of authenticity, numbered" and a foreword by Queen Elizabeth, as well as an album. These additional items, the firm felt, were worth £90, thus justifying the £150 price.

The Authority disagreed. However, they tempered the decision with a statement that the violation of the code was technical only, and that if the firm agreed to stop advertising the collection, there would be no further action. The firm agreed, and the Advertising Standards Authority served its purpose.

73

Would the same have happened in the United States? Our magazines are full of offers of stamps at ten to twenty times what they can be bought for from legitimate dealers. First day covers of current stamps, which can be obtained from Uncle Sam for the price of an envelope and postage are advertised for $4.75 and more. A military magazine in August of this year offered six U.S. three cent stamps showing branches of the Armed Service (Scott about $1) for $17.95, plus $1.50 handling charges. True, one did get a plastic frame with it, but it was hardly an investment at twenty times catalogue, even with the cheap frames.

It is a pity that the magazines themselves are rarely interested in what their readers are offered in their columns, but seldom do they even bother to answer letters. (I have sent dozens of them!) While a certain amount of sympathy might be extended to the sucker who spends $20 for eighteen cents face value in common commemoratives, it is the hobby for which I have concern.

These buyers spend their money thinking that they are not only getting value, but that since they hear on all sides that stamps are such a good investment, all they need to do is spend their money, wait a few years, and then collect their profit from the nearest stamp dealer. By then the buyer will long since have forgotten who sold him the overpriced stamps, and even if he does remember, he will learn that those advertisers only sell stamps, they do not buy them.

So he looks up the nearest stamp dealer in the telephone book, and pays that dealer a visit. It is then that he learns for the first time that he has bought reprints or fakes, as is the case with an advertisement of some Confederates before me as I write. Or he may have bought the 3¢ Maryland stamp (Scott #736, catalogue 20¢ at the time) from one of the well known so-called "Mints" for the advertised price of $2.75, in a cheap frame.

Grist for the mill are foreign first day covers, often bearing the lowest value of a set, with a gaudy cachet and a postmark usually applied in the source's office rather than a post office. (The denomination of the stamp usually is not nearly enough to carry a letter across the room in the country whose name

is on the stamp.) The tariff on this can run as high as $6.95 —
but of course one gets a "certificate of authenticity" with it,
and often an album as well, if payments are kept up for the
required time.

As is the case with inflation, there is little that can be done
about it. Publicity in a stamp magazine is not the answer, for
these people do not subscribe to a stamp magazine, and as
stated, the magazine itself could not care less about the
victimization of its readers.

Please, good friends at the Advertising Standards Authority, how about starting a branch in this country, where your
services are urgently needed?

29   The World War II French Spy Forgeries

To most people, a stamp is just a piece of paper designed to perform a job. To a stamp collector, it is an escape to a distant place and time. But to the brave Allied intelligence forces operating under the very noses of the Nazis in Europe in the latter days of World War II, stamps could be the very essence of life. Without stamps, it could reasonably be argued, the D-Day invasion of Normandy could have cost us immeasurably more casualties than it did.

Preparations for D-Day were made by intelligence and resistance forces many months before the invasion took place. Operatives of many nationalities were secretly dropped by parachute with instructions to contact agents already in France. One of the greatest needs in any intelligence operation is the ability to recognize one's fellow agents. Passwords and secret signs are fine, but the enemy has a way of finding out such things.

It was a member of the British intelligence service who came up with a scheme that was the epitome of simplicity. Why not counterfeit then-current stamps of France, adding to each counterfeit some tiny difference that only someone aware of the ruse would recognize?

This might be a white scratch under the eye of Marianne, the female allegory of France that appears on many French stamps. On another stamp it could be a broader mustache than normal on General Petain or, on still another, an extra bit of shading in the background.

Shown here is one such spy forgery, a counterfeit of the 1939 France 30 centime Mercury definitive, Scott 361. The forgery appears on the left, with a genuine stamp shown on the right for comparison.

There are numerous differences between the two, differences that only spies—and stamp collectors—would be likely to notice. The most obvious of these are the patches of white near and below the right eye of the forgery, as indicated by the arrow. Such patches are not present on the original stamp.

Using these stamps, spies could communicate by mail. The French post office, then serving under the German occupation, actually carried the forgery-franked letters from one agent to another. As long as only the spies themselves were alert to the secret, any letter carrying a normal French stamp could be ignored as a trap, while one bearing British made forgeries could be regarded as authentic.

The Germans never caught on. For more than a year, Allied agents in France contacted each other simply by sitting down and writing a letter. Obviously, each letter was coded, so that if it did fall into the hands of suspicious enemy intelligence, it would appear to be normal business or personal correspondence.

When historians wrote up the invasion, it is doubtful if stamps were even mentioned. Even if the historians did know, it would be unlikely that they would see the significance of these bits of paper that so many take for granted.

Not until two years after the war was the scheme revealed to the world. However, its existence had been suspected much earlier when French philatelists, studying their stamps, found the minor differences in design for which they could determine no logical reason.

Thanks to a large supply of these forgeries having come from British archives after the war, the French spy stamps are not particularly rare in mint condition. However, in used form, especially on original envelopes, they are great rarities. This is because each spy who received a letter with one of these stamps would immediately burn it, to ensure that scheme never came to the attention of the Germans.

Fortunately, it never did. The D-Day invasion was successful, thanks to the preparations made for it by hundreds of American, French and British agents, who had worked for many months to assure its success.

30   Pall Mall (Not the Cigarettes)

*If likeable Robson Lowe, doyen of London phila-
telic auctioneers, ever decided to go the lecture
route, "An Evening with Robson Lowe," would be
an immediate box office hit.*

Most British collectors have heard Robson
Lowe speak, and many in this country as well,
for he seems to enjoy nothing more than showing up at a
stamp club and entertaining the fortunate listeners. His dry
wit, deliberately paced delivery and gift of British under-
statement keeps those hearing him in a continuous state of
philatelic delirium, compounded by the serious mien he
maintains throughout.

I remember his talk at a dinner in his honor during London
'80. With an economy of words, Robbie recalled that his
quarters at 96 Regent Street in London received a direct hit
from a Nazi bomb during the war. The building in ruins, he
took up quarters on Pall Mall, the street famous for so many
of London's exclusive clubs. (Pronounced Pell Mell, despite
what American cigarette smokers call it.)

The arrangements about to be concluded, Robbie was told
by the authorities that a commercial activity as debased as
selling property at auction would serve only to lower the
esteem in which the street had been held for centuries. He
was told to seek other facilities on another street.

Robbie turned to his collection of British covers. He was
sure that he had noted that he had a cover addressed to an
auctioneer, at a Pall Mall address. Sure enough, he was able
to confirm that a gentleman named James Christie had opened
an auction gallery there, in the year 1776. Christie's is, of
course, famous worldwide, and still in business in London.

The surprise was yet to come. This was Robbie's most
unusual way of telling his audience, and the world, that the
firm which he had founded decades earlier had become part
of the Christie organization, and while continuing to operate
as Robson Lowe, Ltd., it was in a position to benefit by joining
the Christie's family.

Later Robson Lowe Ltd. forsook Pall Mall, and its quarters
almost opposite Whitehall Palace, the residence of the Queen
Mother, and moved into buildings occupied by Christie's.

31 The Day Hollywood Discovered Nassau Street

It was P.T. Barnum who said that there is one born every minute, with the second part of the aphorism added by an unknown wit. There is indeed a sucker born every minute, and with the same frequency someone is born to "take" him.

That was pointed out to us while the philatelic documentary film Timbremania was made in New York City some years ago (1979, to be exact). We were privileged to play a part in the picture, telling tales of Nassau Street when it was the center of the stamp trade in this country, in the days before World War II.

A camera crew shooting a picture draws a crowd, even in Hollywood, where film-making is by no means an extraordinary sight. Nassau Street is a narrow thoroughfare, and crowds gathered at the sight of sound men, boom men, and cameramen, intent on capturing on film someone walking down the street, talking.

Although that scene may just be minutes on the screen, it took two hours to shoot. There were constant interruptions. At one time, halfway through the two blocks, a passerby with a portable radio on maximum loudness, passed by. The scene had to be done again. Another time, just as we passed a shoe repair shop, the motors were turned on, creating a loud explosion in the earpiece of the soundmen. And at a luncheonette, a neon sign flashed just as we passed by. And yet another time, the bright sun came out for a brief moment as its rays flashed between two tall buildings, breaking the dull gray of the sky as we passed, requiring a new plan of lighting.

"What's it for?" most onlookers seemed to be asking. The crowd made all sorts of guesses, none of them right, and it did not seem to be our duty to inform them. At one point, about fifteen minutes passed while the shooting crew debated how a certain scene should be done. We were standing alongside a delivery truck, whose driver was on the curb watching.

"What's it for?" someone asked the driver of the laundry truck. "One of them double-oh-seven pictures for Hollywood," the driver replied, much to our surprise, for we were quite unprepared to learn that Timbremania had apparently been given a new name. "Want to be in it? My part hasn't come up yet, but for five dollars I can get you in."

The passerby whipped out the five dollars and gave it to the driver. "Just wait," the driver told him. "I have to drive around the block, so they can shoot me coming up the street. When I get out of the truck, I'll spot you and we'll start talking softly to each other."

The whole conversation startled us, for no way could we see a laundry truck as part of the script that the Penn State College crew had worked out with me. (The film was made for Educational TV by the station in State College, Pennsylvania, with the assistance of the American Philatelic Society.)

The laundry driver climbed into the cab of his truck, telling the sucker to stay at the curb until he came back. (The sucker, smart-like, took down the license number.)

We proceeded with the filming. The laundry truck, of course, never returned. Two hours later, the sucker realized he had been taken when the shooting finished, the picture crew began to gather up their ladders, booms, cameras and sound equipment and the asphalt drilling machine two blocks away began drilling again. ("You are costing the city a thousand dollars an hour," the foreman had told the camera crew when they saw the permit New York City gives for movies to be made in the city.)

Our friend the sucker recognized us. "I have called the police," he said, "And with the license number of the truck I will be able to track down that crook." We suggested that it might be a little difficult to get New York's finest to come on a call of that sort. One can find a mugger in New York in much less time than one can find a policeman.

A policeman came into sight and our friend went up to him. "Let me tell you what happened," he told the officer. "Sorry, buster," the cop replied, "but I'm on my lunch break."

We walked into 116 Nassau, just for old times' sake. The stamp dealers have long since moved out and the building is occupied mostly with insurance dealers. At one time, the glass doors at the entrance of the building had little panels for pushing, each in the shape of a rectangular postage stamp, complete with perforations. They are still there. We took the elevator to the tenth floor and went to the end of the hall, where our offices had been from 1935 until 1946, when we moved to the suburbs. There had been five stamp dealers on the tenth floor. Our first month's rent had been twenty dollars with one condition: the huge safe in one corner of the office had to be removed at our expense. We accepted the condition; it saved our buying one. Our meager stock filled one-fifth of it. We were impressed with the name painted on the safe: "Bogert Durbin & Co." We wondered how many millions of dollars the stamps once kept in that safe might be worth, contrasted with our tiny stock. (For more of Bogert Durbin & Co., read the Scott Specialized Catalogue under the listing for 10X1.)

Our reflections on the stamp business in Nassau Street of forty years ago brought many names to mind. Some are no longer with us: J. M. Bartels, Ezra D. Cole, Max Ohlman, George B. Sloane, Peter Keller, Herbert Reuben, Murray Simnock, Joseph Strauss, Leroy Gardiner, Jack Goldstein, and there are probably many others whom we have forgotten. And of today's dealers, there are many graduates of 116 Nassau: Robert Siegel, Leo Scarlet, Ralph Orton, Lee Gilbert, Meghrig & Sons, Fatoullah & Lazar, and the writer.

We left the building with a bit of nostalgia, a good bit of it, thinking how different the stamp business is today from what it once was.

We were brought back to 1979 with a jerk. Our friend the sucker was still standing in front of the building.

"I called the police again," he told us. "They ought to be here any minute." We walked to the subway, stopping along the way for a sandwich and an orange juice. As we entered the subway, we looked north on Nassau Street. He was still waiting for a cop.

32   Collecting Proofs and Essays

Not infrequently, a newer collector comes upon a United States stamp which is not perforated and is printed on cardboard instead of on the normal stamp paper. Sometimes he is quite excited with his find, and loses no time in proclaiming to the world that he has found a new variety, a rarity, and a valuable item. Perhaps, it is only normal to endow with tremendous value anything which seems to be the least bit different. But in philately this is not often justified.

The stamp on cardboard without perforation is a proof. Making a proof is one of the steps leading up to the final stamp, as we know it to be. The proof tests the plate from which the stamps are to be printed.

A proof also may be made to see how the stamp will look in the various color possibilities assigned to it. Proofs that are bicolored exist for some one-color stamps, as a later decision ordered them printed in one color.

Not all proofs are on cardboard. Many are printed on a very thin paper called india. Proofs even are known on the very same paper from which the stamps are made. In some cases, it takes an expert to tell the final issued stamp from a proof. They may appear identical to the untrained eye.

Many proofs are extremely common. Often they sell for a mere fraction of the price that the very same item, in stamp form, would bring. This is in spite of the fact that in almost every case, the number of proofs issued is far, far fewer than the quantity of the corresponding stamp.

This throws into a cocked hat the idea many newer collectors have that if something is printed in small quantities, it is valuable. The important factor in value is demand, in relation to supply—not supply alone.

Until the early 1890s our stamps were printed by private companies. Various companies competed for the contract, and many times they resorted to devious ways to get the contract, or to take it from a rival company. Sometimes, as happened in the 1870s, the contract stayed only a short time with one company before another took it away.

As one version goes, in 1869, when the contract-holder found it had bid so low to get the contract it could not make money, it induced individuals in many widely separated cities to write letters to newspapers to protest the choice of designs. So successful were the letters that the 1869 stamps were discontinued a few months after their original appearance. They were followed by the completely different series of 1870, the so-called Bank Notes.

A portion of the plate proof for the 90¢ orange 1890 'small banknote' with the notation "Approved 2/8 for color" in the upper left.

These were called thus because the words "Bank Note" appeared in the names of the various firms which held the contract until 1895, when the Bureau of Engraving and Printing took over the job. As long as private companies held the contract, there was little control over the distribution of proofs. Almost anyone wishing to do so could obtain them, simply by asking. Senators and Congressmen were logical recipients, but many stamp collectors also obtained them. Since proofs were not good for postage, the Post Office cared little about them. We occasionally have seen philatelically-inspired covers with proofs affixed instead of stamps.

Some employees of the Bank Note companies were stamp collectors, and occasionally in the past, the old plates were dusted off, sometimes decades after their original use, and impressions were taken from them which ended up in philatelic hands. Technically, these impressions are what we would call "reprints." In many cases they cannot be told from earlier impressions. On other occasions, Uncle Sam brought out similar reprints.

"Errors" exist in the field of proofs, although in the accepted sense of the word, they hardly were issued in error. The 1869 issue, for example, has three stamps which appeared with one part of the design inverted, since they were bicolors, and hence printed in two separate processes. These values are the 15-cent, 24-cent, and the 30-cent.

When proofs of these inverts were issued, undoubtedly under philatelic inspiration, the 90-cent was added to the list. The high values of the Department of State stamps, the $2, $5, $10, and $20, in inverted center form, do not exist as stamps. But they do exist as proofs.

Today, proofs enjoy tremendous popularity. Their doubtful origins usually are forgotten. But many, even today, sell at prices not much higher than what they fetched a generation ago. In some cases the basic stamps have increased in price ten-fold, though the proof price scarcely has doubled.

Many collectors realize this and know they probably never will be able to afford a mint 90-cent 1869. In perfect condition it would fetch, easily, $6,000 or more. So collectors are content to fill that space with a proof which can be obtained for less than a fortune. (1992 retail, $250.) The same applies to the high values of the Columbian series. A proof of the $5, for example, sells for much less than one-fifth the price of the regular stamp, even though they are identical in design, printed from the same plates, but on different paper.

It is, however, quite a different matter as far as proofs on issues after 1895 are concerned. Once Uncle Sam took over, a strict accounting was kept on everything produced on the trail from the original idea to the finished stamp.

Some Presidents, and others, have extracted such things as original artists' drawings, special printings, proofs, and essays for their collections which, when sold, came into philatelic hands. For example, special printings were made of the die proofs the Bureau had on hand. These went all the way back to the 1875 reprint of the 1847 issue. They were said to have been bound into books and distributed to favored friends and politicians.

In 1901, with the Pan-American issue, the Bureau commenced to put a serial number on the back of all its die proofs, in order to control their distribution. This did not always work, and occasionally some did get out without the number.

Today, control is more stringent than ever. On some stamps of the past 30 or 40 years, as few as three or four die proofs were made, and there are many stamps on which, as far as philately is concerned, they might as well not exist.

The collecting of proofs, and their help-mates, essays, is a wide open field for the collector who seeks to collect without great expenditure of funds.

Proofs and essays exist for almost every country which has issued stamps. One cannot generalize about their frequency of appearance or their value.

Some countries provide a supply of proofs for those who wish them. One often can buy magnificent die proofs of stamps of France and French Colonies for the price of two or three packs of cigarettes. They are called "Deluxe Proofs".

A proof of the world's first stamp, the British Penny Black. Note the lack of plate position initials in the lower corners.

For many Latin-American countries, beautiful proofs can be obtained for pennies. For other countries, such as Great Britain, anything in the proof line can cost a substantial sum.

Unfortunately, world demand for proofs and essays has not yet reached the stage where a world catalog that lists and prices such items can exist. In fact, the small supply of proofs and essays available probably will preclude the appearance of such a catalog at anytime in the future.

This may make it difficult for the newer collector of proofs to learn what is available. But it has its advantages, too. It gives the novice a chance to locate and have in his collection an item new to philately which actually could be worth infinitely more than the original cost if bought from someone who does not value it for what it is.

We have said, many times before, but it can't be repeated often enough: in philately, there is no substitute for knowledge.

33   Rarity Versus Value

One fact of collecting that the beginner finds it difficult to understand is the difference between rarity and value. Many things are rare, whether in the stamp line or any other business. But simply because a thing is rare, does not make it valuable.

A letter written by a backwoodsman in 1848, who was killed the day after he learned to write, must be rare indeed, but if no one wants to buy it, it is far from valuable. On the other hand, many stamps which are valuable are not rare.

There is a state in India, now part of the Indian Republic but once independent, called Poonch. The rarest stamp of Poonch is a stamp of which but one exists. It only comes on the market on rare occasions, but about five years ago, it was sold at auction in London. It brought the equivalent of $850.

Yet the 24 cent airmail invert of the United States, issued in 1918, has brought more than $180,000 at auction—although a full sheet of 100 was issued, and at least 94 still exist.

The two most important words, as any high school economics student can attest are "supply" and "demand". Given a small supply, and a large demand, one will inevitably have a high price. A stamp with a small supply and small demand will, in all probability, not have a higher level of price than an item which is in large supply but small demand.

Another concept the newcomers find it difficult to grasp is that because a thing is old, it is not necessarily valuable. The oldest stamp in the world, the Penny Black issued by Great Britain in 1840, is actually a common stamp, although it was the first stamp issued. A single example of it can be bought for less than fifty dollars. More than 60,000,000 were issued.

On the other hand, there are many stamps issued as recently as a year or two ago, or even one which might have been issued just yesterday, which are in such demand that today's price would be tremendous. In assessing value, therefore, the age and the rarity are of only relative significance. Neither age nor rarity in and of itself can ever make for value, without an accompanying demand.

The laws of economics are applicable to every commodity, including stamps.

34 A Philatelist's Castle in Spain

Many years ago at a ritzy banquet in Miami, a midnight supper was served long after midnight. Either to pass the time or to stave off hunger, our dear friend and fellow philatelist, Seymour Kaplan, started devouring the table decorations. It happened to be hibiscus, but ever since we know it only as "Seymour's plant."

In like fashion, the various bits of greenery and blossoms in our garden may have dignified Latin names, but we call them by something that distinguishes them from any other plant. A stately palm known as 'dracaena marginata' may be called that at the nursery, but to us it is Louie's palm. Our one time neighbor, Louie, gave us one and, by careful nurturing, we now have a dozen. Then there is a ground cover we call "Rose's plant". The botanist calls it artillery fern, but that name is a bit too martial for us. We have renamed it after one of my wife's deceased friends, a very gentle lady.

This brings us to "Holloway's plant." If you think that rabbits breed exceedingly well, they have a parallel in botany. I never did find out the real name of the pest we call Holloway's plant, but I can tell you a thing or two about James Holloway.

We were not living in Florida long before Holloway, who operated the local stamp store in Boca Raton gave us a housewarming gift, a potted plant. It soon outgrew the pot, and before long the birds and the winds scattered the seeds. Holloway's plant has been with us since, defying all attempts at eradication.

In Britain, I read that two-thirds of all stamp shops have disappeared. Many are simply out of business, and others moved to rural areas to beat the high cost of doing business by operating from dealers' homes.

No one has come up with similar figures for this country, but there is no doubt that here too the urban ground floor stamp store is becoming a philatelic dodo. And a pity it is, too. Holloway's shop, now a store selling oil paintings, was a convenient stop on my daily bike ride to the post office. There were always a number of collectors; Holloway made them welcome. And just to relax in philatelic surroundings was a great way to start the day.

Jim Holloway died about ten years ago. Even while bedridden for the last two years of his life, he conducted an approval business from his narrow confines. The story of how he first came to professional philately is worth telling, so here it is.

Jim never married. Throughout his youth he had one consuming desire...he not only dreamed of castles in Spain, but wanted to live in one; so about a quarter century ago, he took his life's savings, went to Spain and bought a castle. It was more or less of a derelict, but it was his, all his.

The first thing was to make it liveable. In the course of reconstruction, a locked room was found deep in the cellars. When opened, it was found to have more than one hundred thousand bottles of old wine. (You will have to take Jim's word for this, although Jim ordinarily did not exaggerate.)

Sale of the wine returned the cost of the castle and its improvements. But his good fortune was soon tempered by the events that followed. Surrounding the castle was a small village. In days of yore the villagers worked for the lord in the castle, tilling his fields and making life comfortable. No townspeople in Spain were ever happier to know that they had a new lord and master...and a rich American at that. Their glee was made known to Jim when one of his peons died. The undertaker presented him with the bill.

There were more bills...doctors' bills, hospital bills, and even bills for shoeing horses. When Jim inquired, he was told that this was the custom. When the first baby of his administration came, he was agreeable to paying for it, but all that he wanted was that it be named James. "Jamie" will do, the happy mother told him.

Jim did not mind the living alone, especially since his vassals took care of all of his needs. But one may get tired of living alone, even in Paradise, and he missed the States; so he visited the agent from whom he had bought the castle. It took a while, but the agent came up with a millionaire from Ohio.

Jim asked for payment in dollars, something the prospective buyer would not do. Through some sort of business which Jim never knew, he had amassed a huge quantity of pesetas, and the deal would be in Spanish money, or not at all.

Jim had as much need for pesetas as he did for another castle, so he gave the matter some thought. He had not been a stamp collector, but he read in the paper that Spain was issuing frequent sets of commemorative stamps. A visit to Madrid showed him that the Post Office there would be happy to relieve him of all of his pesetas, in exchange for stamps. The deal was made and Jim came back to Florida with trunks of Spanish stamps, all complete sets in full sheets.

The timing could not have been better. Suddenly Spanish stamps became popular. The relatively small quantities in which they were issued, combined with the worldwide demand, caused prices to zoom. Jim had visits from Spanish as well as American dealers. For years he lived on the proceeds.

And he found stamps to be more than a living. His shop on the main street of Boca Raton never seemed to be without customers. Jim never closed his doors for a vacation or a fishing trip. He enjoyed the business too much. He never told a "time waster" that he had work to do for the simple reason that he seldom did. He did not advertise, he did not do a mail order business, he did not even go out to lunch. Anyone who dropped in was welcomed.

Jim sold his business about ten years ago to a New York dealer who had asked me if I knew of a stamp business for sale. Jim retired, and the shop had a new owner, and for some years was as popular as it had been under Jim's ownership. Came tough times in the stamp business and visitors to the shop declined, just as they have all over the country. New collectors were not coming in and the older ones slowed down or stopped their buying. When the opportunity came to sell out, Jim's successor took it. And now my trips to the post office take much less time, and are far less pleasant.

But Jim Holloway has his memorial, such as it is, and in his memory we are keeping one pot of "Holloway's plant". But when it goes to seed, which seems to happen every other Wednesday, we are careful to harvest the seeds. Thanks, Jim, you meant well, and we hope you understand.

35   Hail to the Fortunate Hobbyist

The endless fascination of philately is unaccountable to some people. Their inability to be fascinated is equally unaccountable to those who collect.

The desire to acquire tangible items not essential to human life is present in almost every one of us. No one would say that the collecting of stamps or coins or anything else is a requirement for existence. On the other hand, the person ridiculing another who does see pleasure in such hobbies may have his own blind spots.

The matron whose arm from wrist to elbow is a fantastic succession of diamond bracelets does not need them to keep warm. She may not admit it, but she is as much a collector as the man who maintains a stamp album.

And the man who has 67 different neckties may obtain pleasure from wearing a different one with a different suit. But actually, none is essential to existence.

We have been asked to defend stamp collecting to men who had a collection of pipes, to others who mounted their piscatorial catches, and to still others who, without realizing that they were doing it, threw as many different matchbook covers as possible into a desk-drawer.

We have seen women who had dozens of costume jewelry effects in the form of a butterfly or a lizard, and others who maintained an entire bookshelf of miniature elephants. We even met one lady who collects elephants, but only those with the trunk in an upraised position!

No hobby needs defending, and we would no more defend philately than ask that the lady defend her collection of elephants with trunks upraised. As a rule, collectors are tolerant of each other's eccentricities.

We know someone who collects campaign buttons only of defeated Presidential candidates. They are far rarer than successful ones; most people save the latter, thinking they may be valuable some day. Buttons of the losers are usually thrown away by their disappointed supporters.

Psychiatrists have long testified to the fact that the man with a hobby, all other things being equal, will be better adjusted than the man without. It was an able philosopher who once said, "Fortunate is the man who has a hobby, for he has two worlds in which to live."

A wartime President, Franklin D. Roosevelt, often said, "I owe my life to my hobbies, especially stamp collecting."

Of course one outstanding reason for their popularity in this country is the constantly increasing amount of leisure time available to devote to hobbies. In many countries the mere act of eking out a living is so demanding of one's waking hours that there is precious little time left in which to indulge a hobby.

Fortunate indeed is the person with the time, the aptitude, and the intelligence to pursue a hobby. Unfortunate is the person whose character, make-up, or time does not permit it.

36   Philatelic Espionage
Uncle Sam Suspects Spy Plot;
Prominent Stamp Dealers Involved.

Do you remember seeing those headlines in your favorite stamp weekly? They never did appear, but they well might have, for it can now be told that several of the top professionals of the stamp business were suspected of working with enemies of the Allies, and were secretly and thoroughly investigated during the war years.

The names, then and now, include some of the best known dealers in the game. The writer ought to know; his name was among them, but then so were some other pretty famous names.

It took more than 30 years for this news to leak out, and if the United States Congress had not passed the so-called "Freedom of Information Act," the whole story would still be buried in the archives of the Federal Government.

The Act mentioned provides that any citizen has the right to demand of his government whatever dossier the CIA, the FBI, or any other branch of the government may be holding. Accordingly, this writer wrote the FBI in July, 1975, asking that whatever records they showed on him be delivered. Clarence M. Kelly, under date of July 7, 1975, replied: "For your information, you have not been the subject of an investigation by the FBI, however, your name appears as a reference in our central files only due to your prominence in the philatelic field.

"I am prevented by law from releasing the documents in which you are mentioned since they include matters that are to be kept secret in the interest of national defense or foreign policy pursuant to criteria established by Executive order...(and)...release of this material would constitute an unwarranted invasion of personal privacy, disclose the identity of a confidential source, and disclose investigative techniques and procedures.

"You have 30 days from receipt of this letter to appeal to the Attorney General from any denial contained herein."

Now this was indeed news! The writer was a bit too old to serve in the armed forces in World War II, but he did do more than his share, helping the War Bond drive and visiting many military hospitals in connection with Ernest Kehr's "Stamps for the Wounded" project. It was somewhat of a shock to know that the FBI was interested in poor little me, when known German spies were running around the country committing sabotage.

The "Freedom of Information Act" sounded very much like the Catch 22 made famous not long ago in book and movie. Uncle Sam would acknowledge the invasion of one's privacy by sharing the dossier on an individual with him, unless it actually affected his privacy, in which case he had to appeal to get it. I appealed.

On August 11, 1975, Richard M. Rogers, Deputy Chief of the Freedom of Information Appeals Unit wrote: "Although we fully expected that the processing of your appeal would be complete by today, it has proven to be impossible to do so as a result of circumstances!"

The "Circumstances" are, of course, well known. The Watergate investigation was in full swing, and the illegal activities of the CIA and the FBI were becoming public knowledge. In fact, the Attorney General himself was up to his neck in hot water, which ultimately was to result in his being found guilty and sentenced to prison for his total disregard of the constitutional rights of American citizens.

I patiently waited, realizing there was no way to hurry things, being especially grateful that at least Uncle Sam was keeping me informed of what was going on. In the meantime, I continued to wonder what I might have done during the war that had made me a matter of concern to Uncle Sam.

It finally came, and now things get interesting. On December 11, 1942, I had received a wholesale list of Bolivian stamps that were for sale by one Guilasava Karbaum, who called himself Casa Filatelica, Casilla 326, La Paz, Bolivia. I recall similar offerings of material for sale from stamp dealers in all corners of the world. They invariably end up in the waste basket, unless they happen to list items of particular interest.

I am sure that is what happened to Karbaum's list. Whether any subsequent lists reached me I have no way of knowing.

I may have thrown the list away, but the Security Unit of Washington had another fish on its line, the writer. Apparently, Karbaum for some reason was suspected of being a Nazi agent in far-off Bolivia, and anyone who received one of his price lists was himself subject to investigation.

Let it be understood that no criticism of the FBI is intended by this recounting of events. The nation was at war; any investigation that might lead to the arrest of any spies working against the best interests of the nation was certainly an investigation that was to be encouraged.

The Government intercepted 33 of these philatelic price lists from Karbaum. Perhaps there were more. We have no way of knowing today, more than three decades later, where Karbaum had obtained the names of those to whom the lists were sent, but the list would seem to be a Who's Who in Philately for the early 1940s.

The appeal granted, the list of 33 names was sent to the writer. It was headed by a collector who turned dealer late in his life, the respected Dr. W. L. Babcock of Detroit. A number of the names are completely unknown to me, perhaps being the names of dealers with whom I have never done business.

Quite a number have since passed to the great stamp club in the sky where all stamps are well centered and unhinged. Two names which will be well remembered by U.S.A. specialists, though they are gone many years, are Arthur C. Lane of Boston, and James H. Raymond of Washington. There was even a publication on the list: Weekly Philately Gossip.

Old timers will recognize the names of other old timers, such as Arthur F. Simonescu, of Hackensack, New Jersey, Nicolas Sanabria and J. Walter Scott, both of New York, and J. N. Clarkson of Ridgewood, New Jersey. From the West Coast, we find the respected name of the United Stamp Company of San Francisco, as well as the late Clement S. Ernst, Jr. of Seattle. Chicago's B. L. Voorhees was there, and Hartford's W. C. Phillips and Company.

We must not forget the auctioneers. There was F. R. Ferryman of New York. Other firms the CIA and FBI looked into were Vahan Mozian, Inc., Scott Stamp and Coin Company, Penny Black Stamp Company (B. Bayer), J. and H. Stolow, Rudy Nowell of Downtown Stamp Stamp Company of Newark, New Jersey and H. E. Harris and Company of Boston.

Canada was represented on the list by K. Bileski of Winnipeg, Manitoba.

Well, it's half a century later now. And we can conclude that among the 33 names there was undoubtedly not one who might be regarded as a Nazi spy, ready and willing to sell this country to its enemies as Uncle Sam feared.

Or should we so conclude?

Perhaps we better not, for at the bottom of the second page of the list of names appears this pertinent conclusion: "Information discloses that 10 of these addressees are very suspicious and that all of their communications require complete investigation."

The names? Who are they? I am sure I was among them, for much of my correspondence during the war was with Britain, as I was perhaps the leading importer of fine United States material from there into the States, as a result of my residence there in 1937 and 1938. But who were the other nine?

Was one our late friend Rudy Nowell? He was rotund and well fed; could he have earned such a fine living just from stamps? Henry Harris of Boston? He showed his patriotism over and over by being one of the most substantial contributors to Stamps for the Wounded. Dr. Babcock? Everyone knew his splendid war record from World War I, as the one person who saved for philately the one cent and two cent A.E.F. booklet panes which might have been used up and destroyed had he not bought up as many as he could.

No, we rather believe that those ten suspicious names were the result of someone's wild imagination. Certainly, had anything ever turned up against a single one of them, we would have known of it long before now—and headlines somewhat similar to the ones that precede this article might have appeared in the philatelic press.

37   It's Time For A Catalogue Change

Sooner or later, the philatelic body politic—as well as Scott Publishing Company—is going to face an issue that is not going to be popular. It will not be the first time, and while painful, it will be in the best interest of our hobby.

The problem is the numbering system as it regards United States stamps, and less serious, those of some other countries. But let us concern ourselves just now with the listing of stamps of our own country.

Over forty years ago, Scott met the problem head-on. It is not too well known that until about 1940, the numbering system of our stamps had been developed in the nineteenth century. That was fine until students learned that there was more than one kind of the one-cent stamp of 1851. Our first regularly issued stamp, the five cent 1847, now properly Scott No. 1, was then No. 28. Various postmaster provisionals took up the first twenty-seven numbers...but not all of them. Some stamps were at one time considered to be postmaster provisionals; others were not discovered until the numbering system had been established. Confusion reigned.

The ten cent perforated stamp of 1856 had been called No. 49. Then it was discovered that there were actually several different ten cent stamps, and to identify them, letters were added. Over the years we became familiar with Nos. 49A, 49B and 49C. It was a little different with the one-cent of the same series. What we know today as No. 24 was No. 42f, and when Mortimer Neinken discovered yet another type, today well known to specialists though not yet accepted by catalog makers, it did not even receive its own number, nor has it yet.

The secret marks of the Bank Notes were discovered long after the stamps appeared, and numbers were shuffled to accommodate them. (For generations, philatelists sought secret marks on the 24¢, 30¢ and 90¢, but had they found them, they would have received A and B numbers.) When the types on the ten cent and dollar values of the 1894, 1895 and 1898 issues were discovered, the numbering had progressed beyond them. Today we put up with Nos. 261A, 276A and 282C.

How many collectors know the difference between "a"

and "A" following a number? The capital letter indicates a major listing, the lower case a minor variety. Scott follows through in its albums by assigning spaces for the "A" stamps, and not most of the "a" stamps.

By 1940 or so, the absurdity of the "Topsy" syndrome, which had grown up as new stamps were discovered was admitted. It was decided to renumber completely all stamps issued up to 1861, picking up extra numbers by cleaning up the Postmaster Provisionals and giving them a separate numbering system. Thus, our first stamp became No. 1 instead of No. 28, and the As and Bs and Cs received their own major numbers. It was a stroke of genius to number them in such a manner that the one cent 1861 kept the number it had had under the old system, No. 63.

Not only were the early stamps renumbered. When our first airmail stamp appeared, few philatelists realized that mail transport by air would grow into the importance it had within a decade. When other airmail stamps appeared, they were moved out of the numbering system system they had had, and placed in a new series, the 1300 series. For two decades, all air stamps were in the 1300 group. The parcel posts were in the 1400 section. Postal Stationery, officials, postage dues, revenues.....each class of stamp had its own numbered area. Who could dream then that much fewer than thirty years later, due to the increasing frequency with which stamps were issued, the Scott catalogue would reach #1299... thus creating a problem in identifying the next stamp to be issued?

Collectors have wondered why there is no #652 in the catalogue. Stamps continued to be added as they were discovered, and removed when common sense dictated. The eleven cent 1922 appeared originally in a blue color, a real, unquestioned, undebatable blue. In 1929, the color was changed to green, and it was given a new number, #652. But the powers that be declared that the new color did not merit listing as a new stamp and it was deleted.

The four stamps of the 1936 TIPEX souvenir sheet were given individual numbers at first, 778, 779, 780 and 781, and were treated as four different stamps, rather than as one sheet. That again left some blank numbers when it was decided to assign just one number, 778, to the complete sheet, and "a," "b," "c," and "d" to the four stamp designs. They were left blank rather than disturb the numbering of subsequent stamps.

As stated, for decades, Scott listed the Postmaster Provisional stamps ahead of our government issue of 1847, making the 5¢ and 10¢ of that issue No. 28 and No. 29. When the catalogue numbering system underwent tremendous revision about half a century ago, our two first government issues became Numbers 1 and 2, as they are today, and all stamps from those to the 1¢ 1861 (#63) received new numbers.

"Topsy" is growing again, early stamps are being moved out of the stamp listings, and Scott may someday have to change the numbers again.

38   Think Twice Before Securing Your Future

To this observer in retirement, "securing a financial future" would require an income of at least $20,000 per year. That is, of course, assuming that the rate of inflation stays where it is, and this in itself is a very doubtful assumption. One of our friends has just sent us a little booklet, produced by yet another of those philatelic prognosticators, which is designed to "secure your financial future."

The most desirable of investments is one in which one's money is doubled, although this little booklet makes "double your money" mighty picayunish. It tells us "one man who spent $200.00 buying some plate blocks in 1972, sold them a short while later for $6,800.00 That's right, a sixty-six hundred dollar profit!"

And the booklet goes on: "Another man wrote me about buying stamps for $50.00, selling them later for $500.00, and being unhappy about it because he could have likely sold them for $5,000.00 if he had held onto them longer."

Wouldn't you like to know what stamps these were? So would we. Unfortunately, the writer does not say. But it could happen, assuming that he could find a dealer stupid enough to sell him some $200 worth of Pan-American plate blocks from 1901 that were actually worth $6,800.00. A dealer like that any of us would like to find, although stamps to that individual would have been a mighty poor investment.

The author of the book, so we are told, is the author of the "most widely read column of its kind throughout the world," although in truth, we have never yet met a philatelist who had heard of him before his ads started appearing in some of our stamp magazines. He is neither a member of the American Philatelic Society, nor of the American Stamp Dealers Association. In fact, we consulted every philatelic directory in our files, and could not find his name in one of them.

The writer attributes much of his expertise to his country-wide staff of advisers, which make up his "network of agents throughout the country...who can get us the stamps we want at the lowest prices. (They are) experienced stamp men, ready at a moment's notice to scour their areas for us." There follows the names of four men, one in California, one in Washington, one in Chicago, and one in New York. None is a member of the ASDA, and the chap in Washington turns out to be in Washington State, not Washington, D.C. as we might have thought.

Of course, not being a member of the ASDA is not an essential to being a trustworthy dealer in stamps, but when we gave the names to four or five of the more important auctioneers and wholesaler/suppliers, we drew a blank in each and every case.

The last time that we heard the rather puerile expression "plate block number" used, it was uttered by someone who had collected for a matter of days. We never expected to see it used, as it was in this booklet, by someone who was boasting of his philatelic knowledge and ability, even if it extended only to picking "winners." The grammar used in the booklet also would earn the writer a failing grade in third term English, with more than its share of sentence fragments, split infinitives, non sequiturs, and dangling sentences devoid of verbs and sometimes nouns.

Those who subscribe to this venture are permitted to enter into a little pyramid club scheme, being told that ready profits are available if one does not want to wait until the "buy" market catches up with the prices you have paid. One simply buys a Harris catalog for a few dollars, and starts advertising his stamps at those prices. Apparently, customers will flock to buy, and since it is suggested several times in the booklet that you buy your stamps at a discount from Harris, your built-in profit is assured. Of course, the "investor" is not told that it is not necessary to pay $50 for the privilege of buying stamps at a discount from Harris. Any auction, and any wholesaler can oblige in that respect.

One has to admit that some of their past recommendations have turned out well, but isn't it true in any market that hindsight is a lot better than foresight? Past suggestions, according to the booklet, have been the Graf Zeppelin sets of 1930, as well as plate blocks of the $5 Presidential and the $5 Hamilton. Of course, it did not take any prophet with a crystal ball to predict that these were good buys. One could make that prediction today, and not be far from wrong. The trick is to be able to buy them at sufficiently below the market as of any given day, in accordance with the basic plan the author lays down. We would ask him how many of the above items were sold to investors "at low wholesale prices, often 20% to 30% and more off their retail cost." If we were sure of this, our check for $50 for the privilege of buying would have been sent long before this.

The best information in the book, and a suggestion no one can argue with, is the advice not to buy stamps direct from the post office with the hope of a speedy, substantial return.

We do love and appreciate the kind words said about men in the stamp trade who are indeed well known, who are called "men of principle and character. Who love the stamp field and what it's given them." (Look, Ma, no subject, no predicate!)

But when it says "Many of them earning $50,000 every year and more" we wonder whether Uncle Sam is going to take a greater interest in our profession than he already does, especially since six or seven well known dealers are mentioned in this conjunction. (And once again, Ma, no subject, no predicate!)

The final page of the booklet assures the reader that "all registration fees received from this book will be donated to children's hospitals or other organizations helping needy children." This is indeed commendable. (The booklet has a price of $20 on the front cover, but this is deductible from the $50 fee required to sample the bargains offered.)

The author indulges in what some people might think is a bit of unjustified conceit, since over and over he implies that his mere recommendation of an issue is enough to make it difficult to buy. (This might be said to be true of the aforesaid Zeppelins and $5 plate blocks, except that he was not alone in suggesting these as investment devices.) And affiliation with his organization imposes a bit of noblesse oblige on the subscriber: "Please keep news of them quiet for three weeks afterwards, so we can line up as many of them for you as we can before word gets out. Because once it does, then it will be too late."

One is tempted to ask why word is given to the $50 buyers before being provided to the "far-flung network of buyers...

professionals who buy for many dealers, from stamp shows and auctions throughout their areas. Ready to get what we want when we give the word. With the know-how to get them at the lowest possible prices." (This "professional" writer must have been absent from school the day they taught the class that every sentence must have a subject and a verb.)

The thought that comes to mind is that the order to scour the country ought to go out *before* the word is given to the $50 buyers. And how much "scouring" does it take to buy plate blocks of C38, and mint sets of United Nations 1-11, which are but two examples of past advice which he says has done so well?

We know a wholesaler who assured us he has over a thousand plate blocks of C38 on hand at this moment; he denied that anyone had scoured him recently. And there does not seem to be any shortage of the first United Nations set. Those scourers ought to go to a New York auction, and their task would be made much lighter.

May we indulge in just one more bit of choice rhetoric? We learn from the booklet that "unless it's a rarity, once a stamp is used, it has little if any resale value."

That will be a shocker to all of us who soak, sort and save the more desirable stamps that come on our daily mail. Just last week, we received a registered letter with a block of the $5 stamp used for postage. One local dealer was happy to part with $2 in order to put it under his counter at $3, where it remained less than 24 hours.

"Little if any resale value?" Perhaps that $3 isn't much to someone who promises a "secure financial future" through putting a few thousand dollars into stamps, but it is still big money to us. After all, we entered the stamp business in 1933, at the bottom of the Great Depression!

39   How We Killed A Collector

"Glad to hear you've decided to become a stamp collector. Friendliest bunch of guys in the world. Tolerant. Unselfish. Generous. Understanding."

"That's what I heard. I was going to collect coins and I went to a coin club. Such politics. Such back-biting. The uncs don't talk to the uncircs. The medal boys don't talk to the token bunch...well, I decided I'd become a stamp collector."

"Wisest decision you ever made. Nothing like that in stamps. We all get along fine together. You're going to collect mint, I suppose?"

"Well, really no. I figure it isn't a stamp until it does what it was issued for, and it seems to me that a mint stamp is no more than a label."

"That's stupid. No one with any sense collects used any more. Sure, kids might, but they soon get over it. What about plate blocks?"

"Used plate blocks?"

"Of course not. Whoever heard of used plate blocks? I just shiver thinking of a plate block being ruined with a cancel. What Society are you going to join?"

"I've been looking them over and, since I am going in for U.S.A., I thought of the Bureau Issues Association. Just seems to have more real collectors in it."

"No one joins the B.I.A. any more. They waste time looking for scratches on stamps."

"Then you recommend the A.P.S.?"

"That has politics, too. Too many chiefs, too few Indians. Conventions. Parties. Travel. We pay hard-earned money for dues and they spend it on parties. Wild times. Whiskey. They take their wives along."

"What about the Trans-Mississippi Philatelic Society? They have conventions in the part of the country where I live."

"They're all the same. Even the officers don't get along with each other. I wouldn't belong to any of them."

"Sure glad you explained things to me. I might have wasted my money joining. I would rather spend my money on accessories. I just bought a Scott National."

"Not a Scott National? No one uses printed pages any more. They went out with hinges."

"No one uses hinges? I just bought five packages of them."

"Our club is considering expelling anyone who uses hinges, or printed pages. Good thing if we can do it. Ever think how many good stamps are ruined with hinges? They ought to lock up every hinge manufacturer and the dealers who sell them, too. I boycott any dealer who sells hinges."

"What about stamp magazines? I was thinking of getting all four weeklies. They say one can't collect wisely without knowing what is going on. Most expensive one is less than 65¢ a week. That way, I can not only keep up with the news, but learn something too."

"News? You see one magazine, you've seen them all. And, as for learning something, all you see is dealers puffing up their stamps and collectors trying to force people to collect what THEY collect. One of the nice things about stamps is that no one tries to influence anyone else. Collect what you want... that's my motto."

"First day covers appear to be booming just now, you think?"

"You must be kidding. Canceling a mint stamp is bad enough, but putting it on a cover and charging extra because it has a cachet? Sheer asininity. No one over twelve collects first day covers anymore."

"You sure have helped me a lot. To think that I might have put my money into used stamps that no one wants any more. And I might have joined a stamp society, or subscribed to a magazine. Close call, wasn't it? I have an uncle who collects. He recommended precancels."

"Precancels? Didn't know there were any precancel collectors left. No sensible collector has anything to do with them. Believe it or not, they wash the gum off their stamps! Did you ever hear of anything as silly? And they even teach the dangerous idea that a stamp that is Perf. 10 is no better than one that is Perf. 11."

"I hear there is a society for people who collect what they call topicals. As a kid, I loved to build bridges, and I always wanted to be an engineer. There are a lot of stamps showing bridges...what do you think of..."

"Pictures on stamps? My gosh. Don't get into that field. That's kid stuff. They break sets, put used in with mint and even buy Iron Curtain stuff. Never could understand what they see in putting a stamp in a book because in their crazy view, they like the picture. And they think they know what they are doing."

"I'm sure glad you warned me against them. I've had some close calls today. But I wonder if I am really going to like stamp collecting. Seems an awful lot of people must be doing it wrong. After all, one magazine has seventy-five thousand subscribers, and the A.P.S. has over fifty thousand members, and the Scott catalogue still prices used stamps, and the American Topical Association has over ten thousand people who do not know what they are doing and probably hate doing it. How do you explain it?"

"I don't try. They're all nuts, that's why. I know I'm doing it right. That's all I care about. Be friendly to all. Collect what you like. That's why we have such a wonderful hobby. You're going to love it, if you get off on the right foot."

"I really don't know if I will. I think I'll go back to that coin club. After all, it's only the uncs and the uncircs who don't get along with each other."

40 Those Good Old Golden Days of Philately

"Did you see this photograph we took at Niagara Falls during the 1892 American Philatelic Association Convention?" The speaker was about eighty years old when he had left the earth and entered Paradise.

"Isn't that young I. A. Mekeel, taking notes, second from the right in the front row?" his friend responded. "They don't seem to have as much fun at stamp conventions as we did in our day."

"You're darned tooting right!" our first philatelic angel said, coming as close to using forbidden words as he felt he might to express himself.

"I notice they no longer hold stamp conventions where they did when we were collecting," observed the second angel. "Now they are always in some big city, New York, Chicago or San Francisco. What happened to Niagara Falls, or Mackinac Island? Do you think that maybe collectors these days do not enjoy each other's company?"

"I remember that 1892 A.P.A. Convention, and the debate we had about the stamps to be issued for the Chicago Fair. There were rumors that the face value of the set would be more than I had spent in any year since I started collecting in the 1880s."

"I remember it well. And when we met at Lake Minnetonka in Minnesota a couple of years later, someone from the Society for the Suppression of Speculative Stamps made a report on the boycott. A chap was at that show with fifty complete mint sets, almost a thousand dollars in face value, and he couldn't sell them at twenty percent below face."

"Just before I died, I was at the A.P.A. Convention at Put-in-Bay, Ohio on Lake Erie. Didn't you pitch for the collectors, in the annual baseball game with the dealers?"

"Yup—I allowed six hits, and we won the game, but then the dealers were getting old and we had youth on our side. Who was it that got that long hit and fell down running to third base because of his beer belly, and got tagged out?"

"I forgot who it was, but I know that I tagged him."

"Remember when we met at Clayton, New York in the Thousand Islands? They had that tug of war between the wives of collectors and the wives of dealers. The collectors won. But the biggest laughs came from the sack race between those who collected British, and those who collected German. But remember...we did not say then that we "collected" stamps. We said we "saved them.""

"There was no bourse then at the A.P.A. conventions. We brought our stamps, and we traded, especially nights when we could not play games, picnic, swim or boat."

"I watch these modern conventions from up here and I don't even remember when they had a picnic at one of them. Now it seems to be all business."

"And I hear from the new collectors coming here that at stamp conventions, you can't even leave your collection around for other collectors to admire. We used to leave our albums right on tables in the hotels, and no one would think of taking them. There are people who steal stamps now... sometimes they even follow dealers or collectors on their way home, and steal them when they let down their guard."

"Yes. That is why the exhibits are now under glass, with armed guards watching, to keep one collector from stealing another collector's stamps. Who would steal another collector's stamps? That is something we never had to worry about."

107

"It even costs money now to look at the stamps on exhibit. Some exhibitions charge money to get in, and if you want to show your stamps, you have to pay for that, too. When we met in the Thousand Islands at Clayton, we paid four dollars a day for the hotel and all meals. A collector just in told me that he had to pay thirty-five dollars just for the dinner!"

"At the 1896 A.P.A. convention, I signed that pledge of the S.S.S.S. not to buy any of the Columbians, but I think that I should confess. I bought a beautiful set at twenty-five percent under face value, and my grandson still has it."

"You make it a lot easier for me. I signed the pledge, too, but I bought a set of blocks from the same guy."

"Do you have any idea how much your blocks were worth? I followed my singles from collection to collection. That was the set that sold in Robert Siegel's rarity sale back in 1982 for $13,500!"

"I could have used money like that, but my blocks were still bringing less than face value when I died. I guess we were both born a bit too soon."

41   Our Friend, The Daily Press

None of our days is complete without the reading of four newspapers, The New York Times, the Miami Herald, the Boca Raton News and what is called a "throwaway," one which can be brought into the house dry three days out of four. Seldom do any carry philatelic news. The Miami paper once had a stamp column each week, but it was discontinued. When I inquired, the feature editor wrote, to tell me that "Philately is a finished hobby."

Our gripe remains with the metropolitan press, although we must once again commend The Times for not falling for any of the claptrap which comes over the wires pertaining to stamps. At least they check the wire stories, for they know by experience that much of what is supposed to pass for fact is pure fiction. In fact, when we read some of the non-philatelic stories, we cannot help but wonder how far astray the writer may have been carried by the misinformation on which he builds his story. Newspapers have long been accused of slanting their stories to mislead their readers to their own peculiar prejudices, but this sin is no less to be condemned than the stupid philatelic news items, invariably based on deliberate lies about value.

Every newspaper which values its reputation should have a qualified person to nix the publication of any story which on the face of it is pure poppycock. A story from the St. Petersburg, Florida, Times is a case in point. It was datelined El Reno, Oklahoma, and we are told that a certain named individual (we know him, so we must be charitable and not quote his name) told the Oklahoma paper that "the stamps could be worth $100,000 or more." Of course, the simple fact is that the stamps are so off-centered that many collectors would not even want to put them in an album, and if that makes for value, then we have been studying the wrong kind of philately for a lifetime.

In California, another of our current stamps turned up similarly off-centered, and one of the major Los Angeles papers which should know better came up with the same $100,000 figure. This lucky finder, in a fit of overwhelming generosity, donated some of them to a charity auction, thus getting double mileage on his publicity. Prospective bidders, so it was claimed, had already offered higher sums for examples of it, and to bolster the claim, the name of a prominent New York dealer, hardly known for his generosity, was given as one who offered $50,000 for one of the stamps.

On October 4, 1971, the Associated Press sent over its wires to every subscribing paper in the country a story on the finding of a complete sheet of a current stamp, entirely imperforate. That much of the story was true, but in assessing its rarity, it added some nonsense that reference to any stamp catalogue would disprove.

"The last full pane of 100 stamps to exist imperforate was the two cent black Harding memorial issue of 1923. This stamp, unfortunately, for the finder, was later issued imperforate, which nullified the rarity and the value."

Of course, whoever gave out this cock and bull story was confusing the Harding imperforate issue with the 1935 Farley issue. The Harding stamps were intentionally issued imperforate for the convenience of those who used the Schermack stamp affixing machines; it was in fact, the last of the Schermacks. It is true that a part perforate sheet of the Harding did turn up, purchased by a Newark, New Jersey dentist, but that was never reprinted. And any collector with even a limited knowledge of stamps knows that the number of fully imperforate sheets of stamps issued since 1923 is a tremendous one. In fact, in 1935 alone, over 75,000 imperforate sheets were issued in the course of the memorable Farley debacle.

We would like to suggest that our philatelic press also be more careful about printing sheer nonsense, for they are only slightly less guilty. The story of the two "finds" mentioned above was carried by several of our magazines, without a word to their readers that the conclusions in the press articles were entirely incorrect; one in fact, and it should certainly know better, is carrying continuing stories about the alleged sale of the "rarities".

42   Panning For Gold in Postal Markings

While collectors over the past twelve decades or more have been actively engaged in the collecting of postage stamps, what started as a sideline in philately is fast becoming its rival, namely, the collecting of postal markings.

For generations these were ignored. How better to explain the deliberate destruction of millions of rare covers, when the stamp was the thing? The miracle is that so many choice covers bearing desirable postal markings exist today. Of course, many of them come from finds made in the past half century or so; not many are known from the early days of collecting, for they simply were not collected in that form.

The most valuable stamp in the world, the one cent British Guiana of 1851, which sold in 1980 for $935,000, was originally on an envelope, or properly speaking (since envelopes had not yet come into common use then), on a folded letter. The original finder removed it.

The 90¢ 1869 United States stamp sells for a few hundred dollars or more, which may seem like a lot of money to some, but it is by no means a rarity. Literally thousands of examples of it are known in used condition. Yet not one single unchallenged example of this stamp on its original cover is known today.

In Iceland, so attuned were the people to the value of stamps that relatively few were destroyed. They were soaked off the letters by the populace and sold to collectors and dealers, even as late as 1910 or 1915. The result is that almost any Icelandic stamp from before that time can be worth ten to one hundred times the catalogue value if still on an envelope; some of the first issue on cover (only 23 are known, and many of these are in a museum) bring $10,000 or more on the few occasions they are available.

An exception in Iceland's case would be postcards. While desirable, these do not bring the premium over catalogue that an envelope with stamps would. For sixty years or more, many cruise and regular passenger ships on the transatlantic run made stops at Iceland. The novelty of being able to send a "Wish you were here" card from such an unusual port was not lost on many. They were sent all over the world by travelers, and they are plentiful today. A business or personal letter from an Iceland resident is an entirely different matter.

A desirable postmark can add immeasurably to the value of a stamp on cover. While our catalogue does a good job pricing our earlier stamps on cover (the catalogue that does this is the Scott United States Specialized Catalogue), no catalogue can list the infinite number of markings which might appear on a cover. Here knowledge pays off. We have discussed in this space before the "fancy cancels" that many of our postmasters used in the past century. The whittler sitting on the Post Office steps was not the legendary character one might think. The chances are that he was the Postmaster himself, carving out of wood or cork a device to be used to cancel his mail, which might tell the world that he was a Mason, an Oddfellow or a Democrat. He might commemorate a baseball game between the Hartford and Bridgeport (Connecticut) Firemen, or he might celebrate Valentine's Day with a cancellation that lay across the stamp, showing a heart with an arrow through it.

Postmarks of course antedate stamps. Our first general issue of stamps appeared in 1847. Manuscript markings, made by the written hand are, of course, known from the earliest days of settlement in this country. The earliest handstamped postmark in this country was first issued in 1756.

One of the greatest finds of covers in philatelic history was that made by the late Philip H. Ward, Jr. in New Orleans, when he came upon the correspondence of the firms of Carroll Hoy & Co., and its successor firm, Buchanan Carroll & Co. It consisted of tens of thousands of covers, millions of dollars in current value. Ward took all of the covers bearing U.S. and Confederate stamps. He left the stampless covers behind as he felt they were of no value. (They were subsequently saved for philately.)

So lacking in interest to philatelists were the markings on our early stampless covers that it was not until about 1925 that a group of collectors united in order to study them. The field of postmarks and cancellations is now a vast field, entirely unto itself. Specialist societies exist by the dozen.

Some seek markings of towns of the Far West in gold rush days. Others look for markings of various post offices when the states in which they are presently located were Territories. There are collectors of Battleship postmarks; others collect mail with markings of Prisoner of War Camps in dozens of different wars. In the early days of aeronautics, barnstorming pilots carried letters on flights, most of which have distinctive markings.

Letters from areas infected with disease were "fumigated" and postal markings applied to explain the cuts and slits inflicted on them to "kill the germs," as though a letter could carry the plague. (No one then suspected rats.) The United States (and most European countries) operated their own Post Offices in China and Japan, and in many other places such as Panama and some Caribbean islands. Most European countries had Post Offices in Palestine. Ordinary postage stamps, even common ones, used for some of these "post offices abroad" can be great rarities when they bear postmarks of the foreign offices, and on the original cover their value can mount to many, many times that given in the catalogue for the conventional marking.

All in all, it adds up to one thing that we have said over and over again: there is no substitute for knowledge. While the newcomer to philately is buying up sheets at the Post Office with a mistaken idea that this somehow is stamp collecting and a good investment, the informed collector is using his knowledge to pick up items of philatelic interest at a fraction of their actual value, for, believe it or not, many stamp dealers today are no better informed on philatelic knowledge than the people to whom they are selling stamps.

43   Let's Give The Judges A Break

It would be difficult to guess how many stamp exhibitions I have judged since the A.P.S. set up its system of giving an air of competency to the selection of judges. While most have been local shows, there have been many nationals and two internationals among them. After listening to the flak that each one produces afterwards, we believe that it is time for stamp conventions to take a good, long look at the rules for exhibiting, and consider the possibility of changes.

Comments, not all of them pleasant, from the losers are not unusual. Complaints from the winners who felt that they should have placed higher in the judging are frequent. Being forced to defend his judgement to an irate collector is one of the most unpleasant tasks a judge has to undergo. (One judge who served with us earlier this year finds no problem at all. When cornered by a disgruntled exhibitor, he always answers, "I wanted to give your collection the Grand Award, but I couldn't convince the other judges to go along with me.")

Such a response may relieve the embarrassment of having to give a more truthful reply, but it only puts the other judges on the spot. Telling a collector that his exhibit was not considered for an award is akin to telling a father that his newborn babe shows a startling resemblance to King Kong.

We are not discussing at this time the competence of judges, a subject which deserves discussion. The American Philatelic Society, in certifying able judges and recommending them to Societies planning exhibitions, took one long step ahead in the history of philatelic competition. But not all Societies are aware of the panel; others are unfortunately located in areas where competent judges do not reside, and the usual reward for a judge paying carfare, hotel and other expenses is a warmed over dish of chicken a la king.

The judge at a stamp show should be what an umpire is at a ball game. Judging is not an adding machine, where the result is the same whenever the same numbers are put into it.

At a convention in San Antonio, an uproar broke out in topical circles when a top award for Topicals was given to a collection that had rated only a bronze in another exhibition. But the judges are supposed to call the shots as they see them, and the fact that there was disagreement does not indicate that either set of judges was remiss.

There are other unresolved problems connected with judging. As a judge, I have seen the same collection exhibited over and over, at show after show. It had not changed a mite over the years. The quality of the stamps had not been upgraded. Errors in spelling still existed. One may debate whether the judges should be impressed with the money value of the stamps or not, but the fact still remains that the chap who has put $50,000 into his collection, under tutelage of a wise professional, is going to come off with higher honors than the one whose funds are limited and that unfortunate fact is too well indicated by the stamps themselves.

Then there is the matter of mounting. The annual competition of the Collectors Club of New York's once was the sine qua non of philately; at these shows, the quality was usually of international caliber. At a national show later in one particular year, we encountered the same collection, exactly as it had been in New York. Two of the judges dismissed it. "The pages are too crowded," said one. "I dislike handwritten pages," said the other.

Happily, the more experienced judges showed the other side of the coin. Had the collector turned his pages over to a professional artist who specializes in mounting stamps, the panel would have been unanimous in choosing his collection. He preferred to do the job himself, and while there was no doubt the professional mounting job would have looked better (and the collector could certainly have afforded it), he was about to be penalized because he wanted to see the job through, obtaining the stamps, studying them, and displaying them according to his taste.

Perhaps most discouraging of all is the effect failing to win the judges' nod has on even the neophyte exhibitor. At a national show this year, a fabulous collection of United States stamps that had been a top winner at Philympia came up against some really fine collections belonging to members of the local club, collections that under ordinary circumstances might have been up in the running, even if not qualified to win top awards.

This distressing situation has been relieved somewhat by the "World Series of Philately" innovation which the A.P.S. instituted at its national conventions. This is a special section for exhibits which had been Grand Trophy winners at previous important shows. By not forcing them to come up against these Grand Award winners, the owners of collections of somewhat lesser merit do not face the same discouragement that might otherwise result. A winner of the "World Series" is indeed a winner, and the owners have just cause for feeling proud. But what if a collection that has not previously been exhibited in other than international shows is placed in the regular competitive section at an important regional show? Should the owner be commended or reprimanded for making it most unlikely that another collection worth being honored is denied the opportunity?

Stamp conventions have changed greatly over the years. We do not suggest that we go back to the meetings of a half century and more ago. They were social affairs, pure and simple. Like now, they were family affairs, but there was no bourse, and no awarding of prizes for the best exhibit in each of several classes. Conventions were not held in cities. They were held at resorts, like Mackinac Island, Niagara Falls, Virginia Beach or Atlantic City. There were tours, fishing trips, picnics, boatrides. If there were stamps sold, it was on an informal basis, with a collector or dealer taking a small stockbook out of his pocket, and showing his gems to interested viewers.

A bourse is fine. Many an attendee today makes his decision as to whether to attend or not, according to the caliber of the dealers who will have booths. The crowd centers on the dealers' stands. An auction brings in the top buyers, especially if it is conducted by a name firm with quality offerings. The only sour note, if it be one, is the unhappiness that results when the winners of the exhibits are named, and the prizes awarded.

Would a philatelic exhibition without any awards be as interesting as one based on the present system? We do not know. Perhaps it might not get the exceptional collections. The late Stephen G. Rich called the breed of collector who took his exhibiting seriously "mug-hunters." And of mughunters, we know many. Does a panel of judges have it within its power to pass over a collection, assembled perhaps a dozen years ago, to which not a stamp has been added in all that time? Should a collection that has won a dozen gold cups be given a thirteenth cup more or less automatically?

We do not know the answer.

We recall one club some years back which approached this problem from a different angle. It sought votes from those attending for the best exhibits. Everyone attending was given a ballot, and the privilege of voting for the exhibit which each individual thought was superior. It did not work. Exhibitors lobbied for votes. There were far more ballots in the box at the end of the show than there were people attending it. Ballot box stuffing had taken place. Show judging by visitors to the show is not at all competent, for how could they possess sufficient knowledge of stamps to compare one exhibit with another on a philatelic rather than an aesthetic basis?

Here is a subject for discussion in the philatelic press. The A.P.S. which has done such a splendid job in uplifting the competitive stamp exhibition would do well to study the matter, and come to some conclusion. A classification of exhibitors who have never before exhibited, a novice class, would be part of the solution; this has been tried on a number of occasions, and it has worked well. A Junior classification is often part of an exhibition; this too has encouraged our younger collectors to participate. The awards given to the outstanding exhibit by a female collector has helped. The Apfelbaum Award, given for the best exhibit on printed album pages has helped to overcome the prejudice that many judges have against printed pages, though the idea behind the award was to encourage general collecting, which has all but fallen by the wayside in this era of specialization. Awards for members of the sponsoring clubs or those resident in the city or state where the exhibition is being held have brought out collections that otherwise might not have been shown. But these innovations, by themselves, are only part of what needs to be done to make the exhibition more representative of the participants.

44   Are You Ready to Sell?

Given that virtually every collection ever assembled will eventually be put up for sale, and that when that day comes, the owner will want to realize the best possible price for it, it would seem that a few words on this subject should interest most collectors.

The truth of the second statement is self-evident. I have met all sorts of collectors and dealers in my time, but I do not recall having met any who would accept less for their stamps then someone was willing to pay. Most often it is the other way around.

What surprises most professionals is that, although collectors wanting to sell their collections naturally want the highest prices possible for their stamps, too often they will not lift a finger to get the higher price.

Whether this is motivated by laziness, or some other attribute I can only guess, but that the situation exists is undeniable. Just ask any dealer.

The most important rule in preparing a collection for sale is to offer it in such manner that the stamps can be inspected. As long as the back of the stamp is as important as the front (and this is not likely to change), this means that the entire stamp must be presented in such manner as to be visible.

Transparent stamp mounts may serve a purpose in protecting stamps against possible damage, as well as preserving the gum. I emphasize the word "may" because there have been products on the market in the past, designed to protect stamps, which actually damaged them. A generation ago, some plastic mounts contributed to the destruction of the stamp, but happily, the manufacturers of stamp mounts achieved consistency in their product, and produced mounts from materials that were known not to harm the stamps or the paper.

But even those mounts that lift with ease to show the back are definitely unpopular with prospective buyers of collections. And those that enclose the stamp, or that risk damage to the stamp by requiring that each one be removed for inspection and replaced, are in many cases going to cause a dealer to tell the seller that he is not interested in the collection in its present state.

The time spent by the seller removing the stamps, and placing them in a stockbook is well spent. True, it does take a lot of time and patience, but if the seller does not want to do it, why should the prospective buyer place a lower value on his time, especially since it may be a total loss, if the collector declines to sell?

In more than a half century as a professional philatelist, the writer has a fine collection of burned fingers — ten of them, the last time I looked — from accepting the word of the owner that "oh yes, indeed...every stamp is unhinged and perfect." Perhaps he is telling the truth, but how adept is he at telling a regummed stamp from one with original gum?

One might suggest a spot check, perhaps examining every fifth, or every tenth stamp. Aside from the additional time involved, such practice is little protection. It cannot determine an exact percentile of the stamps that are not in choice condition. It is not fair to the buyer, if one or two more valuable stamps turn out to be poor, nor is it fair to the seller if they do not.

For that reason, to bring a fair figure to buyer and seller, the collection in these mounts should be stripped of its outer garments, and put in a stockbook where the prospective purchaser can examine both fronts and backs of the stamps without going through the time-consuming process of removing and replacing them.

Complete visibility in a stamp collection is the finest assurance that every stamp being sold will be given its "full day in court", and that all will be valued fairly. Of course, I assume that the intended buyer is a reputable dealer with an established reputation, and not one of the "Highest Prices Paid, $2,000,000 Available, We come to your home" persons. (One cannot warn collectors too strongly not to let strangers into their home to examine their collections. It can lead too easily to a robbery.)

Another common failing of the collector who is attempting to sell his stamps is the gosh awful mess of cheap and worthless debris that often comes along with the albums.

I have been offered collections which came in the most varied assortment imaginable, from cigar boxes, pillcases, polyfilm bags from the dry cleaner, corn flakes boxes—even one in a thermos bottle. (The owner was afraid of humidity, and he found the perfect solution to his fears.)

If all of the contents of this ancillary material were worthless, it would present no problem, but sometimes some items were jammed into the container years ago, when they were not as valuable as today. At that time, a plate block of the "Space Twins" may have been just postage, but today it is a bit more pricey.

Again, if the seller considers his time too valuable to spend the requisite effort to render his stamps saleable, he is simply going to have to pay for someone else's time to do the job, and if it is the time of the prospective buyer, it has to show up in the form of a lower offer.

An investment on the part of the seller of even a few hours in sorting out those cigar boxes will pay dividends. By placing the more valuable items in a stockbook, the buyer can run his eyes over the pages, adding the figures up mentally or mechanically as he goes along.

The statement from the seller "the better items are in this book; the things in the cigar box are very common" will help establish a better relationship between buyer and seller at the very beginning. It is surely much better than the usual approach: "Here are ten boxes containing some really wonderful stamps." With that opening gambit, all that the prospective purchaser will see as he indifferently paws through the stamps will be the skim milk, not the cream.

If the stamps are offered in such manner that they can be examined, it will not take long for the buyer to come to what he feels is a fair price. Getting him to disclose his figure readily is not going to be an easy matter unless (as sometimes happens) the seller has complete confidence in the buyer's fairness and honesty.

It is by no means unusual in the stamp trade, where the majority of collectors and dealers have every desire to play fair in their dealings with each other, for one party to accept the other's price without question — but this happens only when there is a basis, built up over a long period of fair dealing, for complete mutual confidence.

It is my experience, and remember this involves a half century of dealing with collectors and other dealers, that the occasional remark expressed by ignoramuses that "all stamp dealers are crooks" is invariably made by someone who has collected weeks or months, and who got into the hobby, not with the idea of enjoying it as a hobby, but as a means to instant wealth. And when tripped up by his own ignorance, and his own haste to get in and out profitably, the last person in the world he wants to blame for having been victimized is himself.

But ask any collector who has collected for years, and who knows as much about stamps as the chap from whom he buys them what he thinks of his favorite dealer, and you will get a far different type of reply.

45   Philately's Only Billionaire

A billion dollars is a lot of money. So is a million. How many stamp dealers do you know who became not millionaires, but billionaires?

We know of one. And when we heard that he had died, we recalled that we knew him well...almost a half century ago.

It was in the mid-1930s that a Greek-Canadian visited our office on Nassau Street. He had several hundred Canadian commemoratives, including such stamps as Scott 204, 208 and 210. Best of all, he had a smaller quantity of No. 203, which now lists at $13.50 each.

"I don't know if it is worth anything," he told us, "but some of these stamps with words printed on them have a broken 'X' in the word 'Exhibition.' Maybe you can get something extra for them."

We asked him his name

"Pappy," he told us. "You would never be able to spell it, so just call me Pappy."

We told him that when we first met the legendary stamp dealer, Y. Souren, he gave us the same challenge. We had read somewhere that his full name was Souren Yohanassiantz, and we recalled it. We asked Pappy for his full name. It was Pappachristidis.

In the depression, the trains were pretty empty on weekends, and to keep them rolling, they ran cheap excursions. New York to Washington was $3 round trip, and New York to Montreal was only $3.50. There were no stamp dealers in Washington anxious to sell stamps to a new dealer seeking to build a stock, but the United States dollar went far in Canada. We took each excursion to Montreal, and relieved the stamp dealers there of the obligation to hold their stocks of U.S. stamps over a weekend. We even had the dealer most prejudiced against English speaking philatelists, a chap named Daoust, supplying us. A.H. Vincent, Marcel Belanger, and others saved their U.S. for us. Our schoolboy French got a good working out.

Our visit to Canada always included a visit to Pappy. He lived close to downtown, in a very run-down, "walk-up" tenement on St. Denis, just off Ste. Catherine.

We never were able to count his children, for they would run from one room to another, and there was the likelihood of counting the same ones twice. Perhaps there were not as many as our recollection recalls. But we will always remember the stamps. They were in sacks, cartons, bales, barrels, boxes and almost every other type of container that could hold stamps. We never knew his source; one did not ask that. But his flat had almost as many tubs of stamps soaking off paper as it had beds and furniture.

Came 1939, and Canada entered the war. No longer did Pappy come to Nassau Street with quantities of Canadian stamps to sell. The cheap excursions stopped, but we were in Montreal and we visited Pappy's place of residence/business. He was no longer there. But a phone call to a new—and much more prestigious address—found him.

It seems that Pappy had taken his profits from stamps and his savings and he had bought an antiquated oil tanker. He had it put into decent shape, and was leasing it out to oil companies needing ships to carry their product. "It's a lot better than stamps," we recall his saying. "I paid for the ship in just a couple of trips."

During World War II, we saw occasional references to Pappy in the news. He leased his sole tanker to Shell Oil, and his profits multiplied. He leased or bought other tankers languishing unused with their history behind them, and refitted them, and added them to his fleet. He came out of the war a multimillionaire.

We do not recall when Pappy died, but it was a few years ago, and oddly, the news of his death came to me from the late Colin McNaught, a New Zealand dealer, known to many Canadian stamp dealers from his frequent visits there just after World War I. McNaught, whose memory of the philatelic past sometimes eclipsed my own, wrote:

"The first time that I met Pappy was on my first trip to North America in the mid-1930s. I met him in Montreal—I had seen his ads in a magazine printed in Kansas called 'The World Stamp Market,' a publication just for dealers, printed by the people who also did 'Weekly Philatelic Gossip.' I sold him $20 worth of stamps, but he wanted more. He said he did not have the money just then, but asked if I would trust him and give him the stamps. I said yes, and he gave me $10 in American bills."

I seldom read the Wall Street Journal, and would have missed it entirely if a New York dealer who also knew Pappy had not sent me a large ad from that newspaper. At the bottom of the ad was my friend's name—Pappachristidis, not Pappy. His shipping company had gone public, and it was floating something like $100 million worth of stock. He really didn't need the money, for the issue was oversubscribed. "This advertisement is just a matter of record," it said.

It sometimes happens when friends who are ignorant of philately ask politely whether being a stamp dealer can be profitable. When we have been asked, we would usually give an evasive answer, suggesting that seldom did we have to miss a meal, and that our children always had decent shoes on their feet. But a stamp dealer with a yacht? We do know one, but gossip in the trade is that it was a gift from a wealthy father, rather than something earned from selling stamps.

But then there was Pappy. We never did learn whether he had a yacht or not, but he did have a billion dollars worth of supertankers. The Pappachristidis fleet today, we have since learned, includes 12 supertankers. And it is nice to know that in the last years of his life, he was not dependent on his bicycle, as he was able to afford a luxurious car and chauffeur.

The only thing that spoils the story is this: he did not earn it from stamps...but it was the money from stamps that bought him that derelict tanker that set him on the road to becoming a billionaire.

46   Ex-Queen Elizabeth II

In the world of academe, it is the string of letters following the name that impresses...J. Horace Pettifellow, M.A., Ph D., Litt. D. and D.H.L. In philately, we also have somewhat similar honors. When our top philatelists sell their gems, the auction catalog adds to the description such words as ex-Caspary, ex-Hind, or ex-Newbury. Those in the know are suitably impressed. But how does "ex-Queen Elizabeth II" sound?

Don't doubt it for a moment: such additions definitely add to the value of an item. All things being equal, the stamp that is ex-Knapp will bring considerably more than an identical stamp belonging to a collector named Fink.

I never suspected that one of my collections would merit an "ex", and I hardly feel that when I have turned in my tongs, closed my albums, and departed this world, that any of my philatelic possessions will forever be graced by an "ex-Herst".

"Ex-Queen Elizabeth II" has a certain ring to it. Even now, years after its sale, it almost makes me wish that I could have seen it emblazoned in the auction catalog that was used to sell my collection of Great Britain Penny Blacks, Mulready and caricature covers. It was a mighty nice collection, due more to the fact that it was started over forty years ago than to an unusual ability to buy astutely.

You may well ask, and stay with me if you would like the answer, why parts of this collection should, at an earlier period, have been part of Queen Elizabeth's collection, especially since the Queen to date has never parted with any of her philatelic items. She may need her income upped from time to time, and Parliament generally is willing to increase the Royal Allowance, but she has not yet found it necessary to sell any of her stamps, despite the precedent offered by Queen Isabella five centuries ago.

It goes back to 1973, when India was host to its first International Philatelic Exhibition, with a huge exhibit of stamps from all parts of the world. Queen Elizabeth II was invited to exhibit, out of competition, of course. It so happens that two of my books had run serially in India's Stamp Journal, so my name there was not unknown, and I was asked to be on the Jury. Additionally, the judges were asked to show parts of their collections, if they collected, and these too were to be noncompetitive. I chose my Great Britain collection.

India is quite careful in its customs examinations of stamp collections, for as is the case with most countries, it realizes that its foreign exchange regulations can easily be punctured with holes by philatelists. Many of the judges were on the same plane, the fare being courtesy of Air India, but once the plane landed, we never saw our collections until they were mounted in the frames.

The exhibition over, the pages were removed from the frames, passed under our eyes to make sure that they were intact, and then sealed and delivered to the plane, to be turned over to us once we had reached our destination. "You may have possession once you have left India," we were told. "We must make certain that every stamp you brought into India leaves India with you."

My problem was that from New Delhi I was going to Katmandu to meet a collector with whom I had been corresponding for years, and from Nepal, I would have to return to India to get the plane for home. I asked if I would have any trouble getting the stamps back into and then out of India. "No trouble to get them back in," the official told me, "but no way to get them out."

The problem might be solved by my leaving the stamps at the airport, and picking them up on my way back—if they were still there—a risk I did not care to take. Then I saw my friend, Derek Barker. Derek was an official of the British Post Office. He had brought the Queen's collection with him and he was taking it back to London.

I asked the Customs official if I might turn my collection over to Derek who would take it to London and give it to me there, on my way back to the states. The official told me that stamps leaving India would have to be the property of the owner on record with the Indian government. I asked if I might present my collection to the Queen.

"If you let us write in your passport that the stamps you brought to India are no longer your property, but now belong to Her Majesty, of course it will be permitted."

I winked at Derek and he understood. My passport was suitably endorsed. I was much less concerned about my collection's being merged with that of the Queen than I was about its safety if I had to check it at the airport with ordinary luggage.

Derek Barker flew to London, without incident. The Queen's collection went back to Buckingham Palace; my collection went onto a shelf at General Post Office at St. Martins-le-Grand in London. Some ten days later I was in London and Derek gave me my collection. I did not need to examine it. I knew the Queen had not taken a single item.

There must be dozens of better Great Britain collections in the world, but there are not many that included as many items as mine that were once part of the Royal Collection.

Even as I write this I am looking at that old passport. Right opposite my visa for India is a handwritten certification. There it is, permanently recorded, in a document issued by one of my favorite relatives, my Uncle Sam, with the signed statement of a functionary of the Republic of India: "four packages were sealed by the Customs Seal No. 13 and Cld. (cleared) for Re-Export via S/B No. 3 on 23.11.73 through passenger and carried by Mr. Barker leaving by QF 759 on 24.11.74."

"Ex-Queen Elizabeth"... I love the sound of it!

47   A Glove, A Wig, and A Horse Tax

Let's talk about revenues.

Perhaps one reason for their popularity in this country, in contrast to their lack of it elsewhere, is that the early issues are among our most beautiful stamps. The engraving is the equal of any postage stamps, and unlike postage issues, there are few technical aspects to worry about, such as perforations, types and watermarks. (For revenues, that came later.)

Although adhesive revenue stamps were a legacy of the Civil War, actually they had been appearing for more than a century before the ones most widely collected were issued in 1862. As early as 1755, Massachusetts colony was raising revenue with typographed and embossed stamps—and they are not nearly as expensive as one might believe.

The "nuisance taxes" imposed to raise funds to fight the War Between the States extended to items that today escape taxes. It is perhaps a good thing that our Treasury Department does not know that in those days taxes were imposed on photographs, bank checks, express receipts, playing cards, proprietary medicines, insurance policies, bills of lading, powers of attorney and surety bonds. A separate stamp was issued for each purpose (and quite a few more, besides). It was not very wise, and before long, stamps were used interchangeably. Otherwise, it would have cost a fortune to maintain even a small stock of stamps for each purpose.

The odd taxes imposed in this country at that time were nothing compared to what went on in Britain in the previous century. There was such a wide gulf between the rich and the poor at that time that the latter could not be counted on to contribute the funds needed to maintain the world's largest navy, and the world's most widely deployed army. And in order to get all of this money from the rich, only items used exclusively by the wealthy had substantial taxes laid on them. In 1785, a tax was imposed on gloves; at about the same time, hair powder for those gorgeous wigs, so beloved by nobility and magistrates, was heavily taxed.

Then came a tax on horses, especially those that were rented. Very early taxes in the form of licenses were levied on dogs. Carriages were taxed, as were servants. There was even a tax on armorial bearings, for titled families who wished to display them. If one hired a gamekeeper for his hunting lodge, one had to pay a specific tax. Many of these were paid with stamps.

The late George Turner, of Washington, D.C., had a wonderful collection of revenue stamps, especially of the United States, but also including many of these early British revenues. Some enterprising bidder bought a number of these at the Turner sales, and consigned them to Robson Lowe, Ltd. of London. He did handsomely. A one penny black glove stamp, previously unknown in Britain, was in one of the lots in the Turner sale. Estimated at one hundred pounds (then worth one hundred fifty dollars) in the Lowe catalog, it sold for two hundred forty pounds (three hundred sixty dollars)!

Wall Street calls an operation of this sort "arbitrage". Arbitrage is the simple act of taking a commodity out of one market, and selling it in another market where its value is substantially greater. For many years, American dealers visited Europe, regularly taking advantage of our strong currency by buying United States stamps for much less than they were selling here. More recently, when the German mark, the Swiss franc, and the British pound were more in demand than our dollars, dealers from those countries were over here, snapping up bargains.

If postage stamps are too expensive for some readers, why not look into our own revenue stamps? For a very modest sum, one can build a substantial collection of Civil War revenues. Of the first eighty perforated revenue stamps issued in 1862, more than thirty of them catalogue at one dollar or less. Not a single postage issue in our first one hundred forty-five stamps can be purchased this reasonably!

48 An Autographed Earhart First Day Cover?

Here's a trick question: How many U.S. first day covers exist personally signed by the person who is being honored with a stamp?

When one recalls that, except in the case of a deceased president, the subject must be dead ten years, the proper answer might be none. It is rather difficult to get an autograph from someone who departed this earth ten years ago.

But, as with so many things in philately, there are exceptions.

When Amelia Earhart departed on her 'round the world' flight in 1937, she may have carried a number of covers with her. When her plane mysteriously disappeared, trying to reach Howland Island in the Pacific after leaving Lae, New Guinea, the covers disappeared too. Amelia and her navigator, Fred Noonan, were never heard from again.

But, as often happens, there were some covers that did not make the flight. In one instance, Amelia, gracious person that she was, autographed the cover in advance of the ill-fated flight and returned it to the collector, who had opted not to send it on the flight.

Years passed with the signed but unflown cover resting in someone's collection, which eventually reached me to be put in one of my auctions. The time was early in the 1960s, when there was talk of a stamp being issued for the famous aviatrix, who justifiably did not like to be called "Lady Lindy".

I told the owner of the cover that it might be best not to sell it until the stamp was definitely announced, and at that time to send it to Atchison, Kansas, birthplace of Miss Earhart in 1898, and to turn an unflown but autographed cover into a first day cover. This was done.

I do not remember what the cover brought in my subsequent auction sale, but as I recall, it was something like one hundred fifty dollars.

Years later I recalled the story, and mentioned it in an article I wrote. Eventually the tale reached the ears of Robert M. Ingersoll of Vernon, New York. Mr. Ingersoll presently owns the cover.

The path that it followed from the earlier owner twenty years ago to Mr. Ingersoll will never be known, but Mr.

Ingersoll was happy to report that in the auction in which he obtained it, the price was much, much less than the price years before.

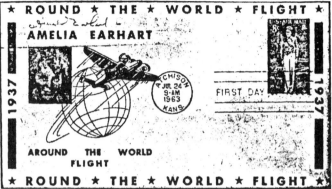

I was unable to obtain a clear photograph of the cover, but if you look closely at this illustration you should be able to see Amelia Earhart's signature, above her printed name in the upper left. The Earhart stamp and July 24, 1963 First Day cancel add the final touch.

So how many covers exist autographed by the person honored, postmarked the first day of issue? Well, now you know of one.

49   The Wahoos of Philately

Every day that passes reduces the number of stamp collectors who knew "Dee" personally. The last I heard his wife was still alive; of course she is one who will never forget the bundle of energy who was often called Oklahoma's philatelic sparkplug.

Dee's real name was DeBajligethy, but from coast to coast he was known as Dee. His headquarters was Tulsa, but he was known at stamp conventions from California to New York—and of course he never missed an APS show.

Dee claimed to be a full-blooded Indian. There was no reason not to believe him. He had the rugged profile of an Indian. It was years after his death that Mrs. Dee told me that he did not have a drop of Indian blood in him; in fact, if I recall correctly, his nationality was Hungarian, or at least, he was of Hungarian descent. A Hungarian Indian certainly would be a novelty.

Dee kept things going. If he was bored at a stamp show, or if things were too quiet, he would let out a yell that might frighten some people, but it told the knowing ones that Dee was there. His favorite word was "WAHOO," and several times a day it would come from his table. His friends would often answer with the same word.

Philately was a much more friendly hobby a half-century ago than it is today. The depression had a lot to do with that. A dealer could get a table at a stamp show for twenty-five dollars, his hotel room cost him five or six dollars and a dinner was not more than two dollars. He did not have to sell more than one hundred dollars worth of stamps in three days to make it pay; usually he was more interested in a good time.

There were a number of informal clubs in those days. The stamp club in Ravenna-Kent, Ohio formed a group called the Visiting Firemen of Philately. One had to attend three stamp shows more than one hundred miles from home to qualify for membership. Once qualified, the dealer was invited to a dinner where a feature was an initiation ceremony in which the new member ended up with a pitcher of water being poured down his pants while he was trying to pop a coin from his forehead into a cup. Dues? There were no dues. The new members picked up the tab for dinner, and they were then members for life. Is it any wonder that the VF of P became the fastest growing stamp group in the 1930s? (The VF of P became national when its largest meetings were during APS conventions.)

The feminine gender was not as well represented in active philately then as it is now. The wives came to conventions, but they went to fashion shows, shopping tours and bridge parties. None was welcome to one of the male fun groups; it remained for the wives of SPA officers (Society of Philatelic Americans) to form the "W.W.s" The great secret the W.W.s maintained was what the initials stood for. All of us assumed they meant "Wild Women", but when anyone asked, a Mona Lisa-like smile was the only answer.

Dee had his "Wahoo" Club, and it had one advantage over all of the others: an emblem of membership that Dee provided at his own expense. The late Ingeborg Herst, who died in 1954, was a member of the Wahoos with me; Dee did not draw the line at allowing ladies to join, as did the other fun groups. On Mrs. Herst's death, I forwarded her membership medal to the Oklahoma Philatelic Society.

The OPS was the society dearest to Dee's heart. His ambition was to have one of the two large national societies hold its convention in Oklahoma, and had the war not come along in 1941, he would certainly have been successful. But Dee's vision went beyond a national society; he foresaw a worldwide group of philatelists that would meet all over the world...and he almost succeeded.

It was to be held first in Tulsa, then the world. The first convention of the "Worldwide," as he wanted his society to be known, opened in Tulsa, Oklahoma in May, 1939. Dee tried to have the U.S. Post Office honor his show with a commemorative stamp. The APS had been honored with a souvenir sheet, both in 1933 and 1934 (Scott #730, #731, and #750). A souvenir sheet also was issued for a regional society meeting in Omaha in 1934 (#751).

The USPO was so bombarded with requests for souvenir sheets that it announced there would be no more. The SPA, second largest society in the country then, protested the ruling and the Post Office agreed to make an exception (#797, in 1936). A souvenir sheet was issued in between, in 1936, for TIPEX (#778), and the Post Office then announced the policy it has since followed: there would only be souvenir sheets for international shows, held at approximately ten year intervals in this country.

Dee could not get the ears of the right people, to make an exception, but he did the next best thing. He convinced our neighbor to the south that great things were happening in the U.S., and Mexico agreed (see Scott #C94-96). The set of air mail stamps reproduced the subject that Dee recommended, the statue of the Pioneer Woman at Ponca City, Oklahoma. Scott errs in calling it the "World Philatelic Convention." Dee preferred the word "Worldwide."

Just why Detroit was selected for the second meeting of the Worldwide we may never know, but in 1940 it was held there. The lengthening shadow of World War II was already spreading over this country, although Pearl Harbor had not yet occurred. But transportation difficulties connected with "defense"—the U.S. had suddenly realized its unpreparedness for war—caused the show to be sparsely attended. It was the death of the Worldwide. Even the APS found it impossible to hold a convention in 1943.

Philately, at least insofar as its conventions are concerned, has never been the same. I have often wondered what would happen if Dee were suddenly to come back to this earth and attend one of them. He would probably find it too sedate, too given over to business, too much lacking in the fun and fellowship that was so intrinsic in the hobby in which he had played a part.

But one thing I do know: that non-Indian voice would blare out the word he liked best—"WAHOO!"

And then he would smile, extend that hand he offered to everyone in friendship, and tell you that he was the only full-blooded Indian in the stamp trade.

Almost everyone believed it. Including me.

50 You Can Call Me Noble, You Can Even Call Me Schepen

Our Declaration of Independence might say that all of us were born equal, but the caste system certainly applied in Germany until quite recent times, and when Germans addressed their envelopes, they might have different ideas: Some were born higher than others.

The expression was "Wohlgeboren", which means "high born". But to be high born was not enough; some people were even one step higher. The title "hochwohlgeboren" before the name of the addressee is not at all unusual. The wife of a medical doctor is automatically as "highborn" as her husband, as the title could be used on the wife as well.

The addresses on old covers are always fascinating. The most incredible title that I have ever seen on a nineteenth century cover was on a Sea Letter, sent by our own Department of State in Washington for ship captains to carry with them when they visited foreign ports. This sea letter had the following titular address, in four languages, English, French, Spanish and Dutch, dated during the administration of President Abraham Lincoln:

> "Most Serene, Serene, most Puissant, Puissant, High, Illustrious, Noble, Honorable, Venerable, Wise, and Prudent Lords, Emperors, Kings, Republics, Princes, Dukes, Earls, Barons, Lords, Burgomasters, Schepens, Counsellors, as also Judges, Officers, Judiciaries, and Ecclesiastical or Secular . . . etc., etc."

If this custom prevailed today, some of those speeches at the United Nations would be even longer than they are.

But it's that word "schepen" that staggers us. We hope Lincoln knew what it meant. We have not found it in any of our dictionaries.

135

51 On International Philatelic Cuisine

Israel is a wonderful country to visit. Just to see how an industrious group of people have taken a land abandoned by the Arabs as useless, and made of it a veritable garden is something wonderful to behold.

But even in a garden the food isn't always as desirable as it might be, especially to someone who is reluctant to become enthusiastic over kippered herring, tehina, and hoomus. The last two foods are Arab-inspired, and staples of the Israeli diet. If there were no other reasons for the Israelis to dislike the Arabs, these two foods would be ample cause.

After some two days in Israel, we wanted nothing so much as a dish of bacon and eggs, and a good American steak. After one week, even the need for a typewriter took second place to those gustatory delights we Americans so often take for granted. We were determined to do something about the situation at the earliest opportunity.

Our next stop was Naples, and after an arrival there late at night with a nondescript evening meal on the Alitalia plane, we set the alarm clock for early arising to get a good solid meal. We found only a milk bar open at that early hour, and with our most limited knowledge of Italian, we tried to plan the meal for which we had waited a fortnight.

"Uova?" we inquired of the chap behind the counter. He shook his head. He had no uova. But sensing our disappointment, and perhaps realizing that I was the first patron of the day, he summoned an urchin playing nearby to run across the street. The ragamuffin came back clutching an uova in each hand. Not knowing enough Italian to specify how we wanted the uova fixed (what can they do wrong with two eggs?) we tried to decide what to order while the uova were prepared. We saw a large pile of juice oranges: our phrase book assured us that if we said "orang-ee" that any Italian would know we wanted orange juice, and it worked. Another employee tackled the oranges.

The sign on the wall read "Nestle's Schokolade", which almost anyone deficient in Italian might understand. We read the sign, aloud, and the third counter clerk took out the hot water and the dry powder, and went to work.

Still with nothing on the table but silverware, we watched each man busily engaged preparing the eggs, the juice and the hot chocolate. It wasn't quite the gourmet treat we had been anticipating, but it certainly beat herring. Then suddenly it happened. The uova man poured his two well stirred raw eggs into the freshly squeezed orange juice, and that concoction was poured into the malted milk mixer which was about to prepare the hot chocolate.

The elixir was served in a tall glass, with the three Italians standing next to the table anxiously awaiting our comments once we had sampled the unpleasant gooey mess. We rose to the occasion, and smiled. "Bono, bono", we reported. We consumed it to the last drop. The three men went back behind the counter, happy that they had done so well with what must be the latest American recipe for a hangover.

At that, it was better than anything we had served to us in Israel!

52 Understanding Unusual Postal Markings

A collector in Minnesota has described to us a cover which he received from the United States Consulate in France. It bears a French stamp. But the French stamp had been canceled in Washington, D.C., and there are no French postmarks on the cover. Instead, it bears a two-line handstamp in purple which reads: "This article originally mailed in country indicated by the postage stamp."

Actually, the wording may vary a bit from that given, for there are many types of this handstamp, and it has been in use for quite a number of years. Briefly, it is diplomatic mail, carried out of the mails from France to this country by a diplomatic courier. If it were official mail, perhaps from the Consulate to the Department of State, it would simply be carried to Washington, along with other messages, dispatches, and papers, and delivered by Government messenger, or by official mail, to the destination.

But if addressed to an individual, custom and Universal Postal Union regulations require that the stamp of the country in which the letter originated be placed upon it, even if it is not consigned to the Post Office in that country.

In the case mentioned, the letter would probably get more prompt treatment when carried by courier to Washington, and posted there, than if originally posted in France. On being deposited in the Washington Post Office, the French stamp (or the stamp of any other country, as the case may be) would receive the normal Washington cancel, and follow ordinary mail channels to reach its addressee. The two line purple handstamp explains the apparent anomaly of the U.S. Post Office's granting the facility of the United States mail.

This is just one instance where one may find the very clearly applied postmark of one country on the stamps of another. While far from rare, such letters are always out of the ordinary, and they always add considerable luster and spice to a collection.

Although there are far fewer Transatlantic liners than there once were, and though few of them today carry the extensive postal facilities they once did, ship's mail can also produce the postmark of one country on the stamp of another.

Another unusual marking. This partial cover shows a U.S. 1¢ 1857, used from England to Maine. In this case, the stamp was cancelled by an 1859 Cardiff (Wales) "162" cancel, and carried by British packet boat (per the circular cancel in the lower left). But the cover was treated as unpaid, since an American stamp was used for regular mail from England. (Note the light manuscript "Due 24 cents" in the upper left.)

Before the advent of the airplane, when Transatlantic mail was carried only by ship, each liner carried a full component of postal workers. Thousands of sacks of mail destined for foreign countries were delivered to a ship just before sailing.

The mail was "worked" as the ship proceeded, and by the time it reached port on either side of the Atlantic, the mail had been sorted, sacked, and marked so that it could proceed to its destination without any loss of time.

Performing this job while the ship proceeded at 15 knots an hour could save days over the old system of sorting the mail on land, before the ship's departure. In those instances, of course, letters were usually canceled in the American, British or German Post Office, as the case might be, before departure.

However, a passenger on an American ship heading for Britain might decide to write a letter while at sea. An American stamp would be called for, since the ship was actually a little bit of American soil, but without an American Post Office in which to deposit the letter, it would be mailed aboard the ship, to be taken to the nearest Post Office in the country which the ship reached first.

This would be a "paquebot" letter, to use the French term, and usually the postmark would include that word somewhere, occasionally with the name of the town where the mail was deposited, or sometimes added to the cover with another postmark.

Some collectors confuse the term "paquebot" with "packet boat." In the philatelic understanding of the terms, they are completely different.

A "paquebot" letter, as explained, is one mailed at sea, posted on the ship, to be turned over to a Post Office at the ship's destination, and the nationality of that office may differ completely from the country which issued the stamp.

A "packet boat" cover is one carried on a ship which possessed a mail contract to carry mail. This term is usually (but not exclusively) reserved for the ships which plied our lakes and inland waterways, carrying the mails on contract for the Post Office Department.

In most cases, their letter-carrying activities were advertised to the world in the form of a special cancelling device, sometimes with only the name of the steamer but occasionally with the name of the Master, the firm operating the line, and even its weekly schedule.

While most of these Packet Boat covers are from ships plying the Mississippi River, and its two main tributaries, the Missouri and the Ohio, such covers are also known from the Red River, the Tombigbee, the Alabama, and several others. Among the rarest of packet boat handstamped markings are those from the old stern-wheelers which operated on the Columbia River, in the Pacific Northwest.

53   Affordable Rarities

In English, the word is "Specimen." In Spanish, it is "Muestra." And in Italian, it is "Saggio."

Many years ago, a dealer who was sadly lacking in philatelic fundamentals asked us to help him find the Italian island of Saggio. "Somewhere in the Adriatic," he suggested.

Specimen stamps have until recent years been among the orphans of philately, steadfastly ignored by all but specialists. British and Colonial stamps overprinted (or perforated) "Specimen" once could be picked up with ease at from one-tenth to one-twentieth of their nominal catalogue values. Things are changing.

In the 1920s and 1930s a chap named Arnold Herrman, a wealthy commodities broker on the New York Produce Exchange, embarked on the task of building a collection of British specimens. It was an endless task of course, but Nassau Street was pleased to accommodate him. He made the rounds daily; specimen stamps had no buyers and even though he frankly said he was not overpaying, he did amass a large collection.

"Some day they will be appreciated," he often told us. And he surely was right. The only problem was that his parents timed his birth very badly. He died a quarter century before they came into their own. And the market has been skimmed clean.

Whether the stamp says, "saggio," "muestra," or "specimen," the reason for the overprint is the same; the stamp was not indicated to be used for postage. It may have been a gift to a visiting postal dignitary; it may have been a sample sent to the master stamp collection maintained by the Universal

Postal Union in Berne; it may have been an example of a stamp sent out for publicity, or for illustrative purposes, or even to a prospective bidder on a stamp issue.

The Republic of China regularly issues Specimen stamps, which it sends to philatelic correspondents to illustrate their new issues. To assure that the mint stamps will not ultimately find their way back to Taiwan to be used to the detriment of the Postal System, each is subjected to overprinting, with the figures or denomination on the stamp covered with black bars.

The collecting of United States Specimen stamps is engaged in by relatively few collectors. Some of them have been doing it for years; anyone starting now is going to have trouble getting anywhere. How would you like to be starting a new field of collecting, and learn that the original issue quantity of three items you are going to need runs from 7 to 12? Just how many exist today is problematical. (Reference is made to the $5, $10 and $20 State Department Special Printing specimens, Scott O69S-O71S.)

There are at least nine different types of Specimen overprints that appear on United States stamps. These nine are identified as Types A through I and are illustrated in the Scott Specialized U.S. catalogue.

Actually, there are more than nine, but so little is known about the others that Scott takes a quizzical look at them, especially those which are unique. The three stamps of the 1918 air mail issue exist with a Specimen overprint in block capital letters; the same overprint exists on the green and black $5 Franklin stamp (Scott 524). All four of these "leaked" out of Switzerland, where the story was that un-overprinted stamps were substituted for them. Because of their cloudy background, they brought very little in a New York auction. If records of their authenticity or additional specimens ever turn up, they may achieve catalogue recognition. (It is doubtful indeed that even when they were less valuable than now, someone would render a saleable popular stamp into one that no one would purchase, but it is not inconceivable.)

A dealer in Spain once submitted to us for purchase a short set of the 1902 issue, composed of several values between the 1¢ and the 10¢, each stamp overprinted "Ultramar," which is the Spanish word for "Foreign." They did not enjoy Scott catalogue recognition. When queried, he admitted he knew very little about them, except that they had been sent to the Spanish Postal Administration on their appearance in 1902, and the Spanish apparently overprinted them for the state collection.

They eventually ended up in the famed 1902 collection of the late Dr. Robert Breakey of Lansing, Michigan. When sold with the balance of his collection about 1970, they brought disappointing prices, once again proving that a listing in the catalogue is essential to philatelic acceptance.

Aside from the overprints that read "Specimen," Uncle Sam has put out a number of other items that fit into this field. The later Bank Note issues were overprinted Sample and Sample A for distribution to prospective bidders for printing contracts for our stamps. To assure that they were not to be used as postage stamps, some denominations were intentionally printed in a color not used for the normal issue, and a startling variation from the ordinary they are. The 2¢ comes in various colors besides the conventional red brown, including lake and scarlet. The 10¢ comes in green as well as brown, and the 15¢ in blue as well as orange. A 90¢ in blue seems to be quite an improvement over the normal issued in carmine.

If one is unfamiliar with these most interesting issues, he will wonder just how expensive they are. This is the very point of the article. So little in demand are these that catalogue quotations are little more than nominal; the color variations mentioned above list in the Scott Specimens section at $75.00 each, and their actual value is so much less than that, that auctioneers have to group several together to make a lot of sufficient value to warrant the listing. Condition is seldom a problem; the Sample and Sample A specimens generally come well centered, with full gum and unhinged.

Only a handful of collectors know the full story of the Official stamps overprinted Specimen. These stamps, 96 in number, are not specimens in the proper sense of the word.

1¢ Agriculture Special Printing with SEPCIMEN error overprint

They are Special Printings, and are carried in that section of the catalogue. They were made at the same time, and for the same reason that the 1875 Special Printings were made. (The reason? You tell me. The story that they were made for and put on sale at the 1876 Centennial Exhibition in Philadelphia is a fairy tale that does not die.)

Alone of the Specimens, the Officials have been more widely sought than any of the others, especially among those who are aware of their proper status as Special Printings. But this small number of collectors, while they have boosted catalogue values in recent years on those stamps of which only a handful exists, have been able to do nothing about those of which a nominal amount was issued. The 7¢ War (now Scott No. O87S D) was issued to the tune of 539 copies. Perhaps half are in collections today: the price ascribed to it is $40.

One day collectors will wake up. We smile at those who tell us that the collecting of U.S.A. stamps is too expensive. We heard that when one could buy a $5 Columbian for $10, and we hear it now that they cost a hundred times that. Nothing is further from the truth. Collecting what is in greatest demand can be expensive; that is why movies cost more on Saturday night than on Monday afternoon.

There is one more field of U.S. specimens which should be mentioned, although these are so rare that perhaps 95 percent of all collectors have never seen one. In 1897, the Universal Postal Congress was held in Washington, and as a souvenir, each delegate was given a boxed gift. It consisted of one each of the then current envelope and postal cards, as well as a set of the then in use 1895 issue, the 10¢ special delivery, the six postage due stamps, and the 12 Newspaper stamps, Scott PR114S O to PR125S O. (A complete set of the latter, which is so rare that it comes up at auction perhaps once in ten years, catalogues at $1,020.)

In connection with these stamps, we recently heard an interesting story. As most students know, one plate of the $1.00 1895 stamps contains three rows of stamps that are Type II, the balance being Type I, which is somewhat more common. When the U.P.U. Congress stamps were overprinted, by chance this was the plate selected for overprinting, so three rows of the pane were Type II. In other words, for every seven Type I stamps, there were only three Type II, and to put together a complete set with both types would be difficult indeed.

A well-known dealer, in conversation with one of New York's top auctioneers, offered a wager that he owned a stamp, cataloguing less than $200 at the time, and listed in the U.S. catalogue, that the auctioneer had never seen, never owned, and never offered in one of his sales. It seemed a sucker bet, but the auctioneer accepted, not knowing that the stamp that was subsequently shown him was what was then listed by Scott as 276A-S O. The owner of the stamp won the bet; the writer does not recall ever having seen the stamp come up at auction, nor even seeing it in an exhibit. Today it lists in Scott for $450.

Collecting United States is too expensive, you think? It isn't, but to collect in a rewarding field such as Specimens takes clever detective work, a good deal of time studying catalogues and advertisements, plenty of legwork, and happily not always too much money.

54   Foreign Aid, The Philatelic Way

Stamp collectors must be about the most generous people in the world. Dozens of nations have found this out, and manage to issue stamps to cover all of their expenses, thereby being able to dispense with such unnecessary things as taxes and duties and fees.

Andorra, a country high in the Pyrenees between Spain and France, has supported itself for decades from the sale of stamps. When Scotch was $1.50 per quart, and cigarettes 25¢ per pack in Andorra, it was simply because such things did not need to be taxed.

Monaco made a tidy living for Princess Grace and Prince Rainier by issuing sets of beautiful stamps regularly, the revenue from which the royal couple lived in style. When revenue from the gambling casino which kept Monaco running fell off, stamps made up the loss.

Commander Byrd's first trip to Antarctica, made in the depression, could not be made from Federal Funds, so the Post Office issued a three cent stamp which was to be used on letters Byrd took to the South Pole. Uncle Sam charged 50¢ for each letter; it paid for the trip.

Liechtenstein, a country in central Europe, makes almost as much from its stamps as it does from licensing corporations to do business there. There is a distinct advantage to owning a Liechtenstein corporation. One pays no taxes on its profits. The lawyers and bankers there are among the wealthiest in the world, as they spend their time forming corporations and forwarding mail.

San Marino, the oldest republic in the world, is surrounded by Italy but independent...so independent that every night at sundown they used to lock the country up and all foreigners had to leave. The gift shops opened up the next morning for the tourists, though. There were no taxes then; the beautiful stamps they issued supplied all of the needs for the country.

Sometimes individuals even think up non-existent countries, print stamps for them, and hope that the stamp collectors will buy them before they read in the stamp magazines that they are frauds. Years ago it was the country of Ocussi-Ambeno. There really is such a place. It is part of Timor, an island which Indonesia seized from Portugal, but the latter, having troubles of its own, forgot to complain about it. Two New Zealand youngsters were behind the racket, and even though they pocketed many thousands of dollars from the scheme, the New Zealand police joined them in a good laugh when Indonesia filed a formal complaint.

There is an uninhabited island off the Scottish coast called Staffa. Its owner sold a London joker the rights to issue stamps for it for a nominal sum. Great Britain would never allow something of this sort to happen, but the issuer was careful to advertise the stamps only in the United States. He printed them on paper he claimed was made from solid gold, and he made the denominations high enough to become wealthy. He admitted that if he had found enough buyers in this country to buy his wares, he would have taken in Eighty Million Dollars! Someone was unkind enough to send the Laird of Staffa a newsclipping with this remark in it, so the Laird sued in London for a piece of the action.

Although the 1976 Olympic Games left Montreal in debt, and lost money for the organizers, were it not for their portion of the money raised by the sale of Canadian stamps, matters would have been a whole lot worse. Tickets sold amounted to $27,000,000. The television rights were sold for $32,000,000. The sale of commemorative stamps and coins amounted to $90,000,000.

Uncle Sam is not unmindful of the gold that lies in them thar philatelists. If you have seen the spot ads on television plugging the hobby of stamp collecting, do not think for a minute that it is a waste of taxpayers' money. Back in 1976 the advertising budget was set at $250,000; philatelic sales were estimated at $50,000,000. Philatelic sales still may be the most profitable activity in which the federal Government ever interested itself, especially since most of those stamps will end up in albums and folders, with the Postal Service never called upon to give service for them.

It costs Uncle Sam under $2.90 per thousand to print commemoratives and he currently sells them for $290 per thousand. With a markup like that, even a Gucci would be happy.

55 A Language All Our Own

There has been a mighty unusual language in the making among philatelists. It is a sprightly tongue, one that makes perfect sense to the initiated, but one that can be mighty confusing to the non-collector. Just as an example, let us listen to this conversation between two stamp wives in their husbands' absence.

"Have you noticed, Marge, how our husbands' language has changed since they took up stamp collecting?"

"I should say I have," replied Marge. "John never uses slang, but whenever he looks at your husband's stamps, he repeats over and over 'oh gee, oh gee'. It gets tiresome."

"Yes, I know. Henry tried to explain to me that mints are the best investment, and you should have seen how he looked at me when I reminded him that the doctor said he must leave all kinds of candy alone."

"John lost his temper completely when I came home the other night and found him soaking his stamps in oil. He said he was looking for watermarks. I told him if he wanted to see watermarks, he could see several where he put his drink down on the dining room table."

"It is nice to know how far back their friendship goes, but now I worry when they go out to the stamp club. As they went out the door, Henry said distinctly that he expected to get a merry widow before he came home. John told him he thought he would be able to pick one up at the club."

"And I am wondering what they meant when they said that they were going to hear a talk on blackjacks. Why in heaven's name would they want to know about blackjacks?"

"I'm sure I don't know, but when they came home from the club last week, I thought they were going to fight. They had bought a sheet of stamps, and just when they were about to start determining its value, Henry said to John 'you can get your face out of the straight edges'. Imagine! He told him where to put his face—and John didn't even get angry."

"Do you think this stamp collecting thing is maybe getting to them mentally? Just last night, Henry showed me an imperf pear. You know we have that Bartlett pear tree and I thought he had developed a new kind of pear. But it wasn't a pear at all. It was just a stamp without any holes."

"This whole stamp thing is crazy. John had some big stamps that he said were revenues, and it said in the big book that they were very rare with sewing machine perforations. I try to take an interest in this stamp thing, so when he was at work, I decided to surprise him. I was very careful how I did it, but I put the stamps through the sewing machine. I was even careful to make them what John calls 'well centered.' But did he thank me? No—he said that I had ruined them. How could I ruin stamps by making them rarer?"

"Henry came running into the house the other night, went right to the phone, called up John, and asked if his new cat had come. Apparently it had, for Henry said, 'Quick, John, let me know what the cat did to the broken hat.' Now that's so silly. I know you don't have a cat because of John's asthma, and I don't think I have ever seen either of them with a hat."

"I won't even look at John's stamps after what happened the other day. He bought a block of the red Lincoln stamps for twenty dollars, and he told me that if they had been on blue paper, they would be worth a thousand dollars, instead of just twenty dollars. I wanted to surprise him, so I took some blue dye and I did a very good job with them. I was surprised to see the glue come off, but I hoped that John would be so excited to see the blue stamps that he wouldn't notice it. I dried them and propped them up at the dinner table when he sat down to eat. He didn't notice them until dessert, for he was reading the evening paper, but you should have heard him when he saw them. Now he is taking the twenty dollars out of our vacation money!"

"I never thought Henry would show such partiality with our children, for we agreed many years ago to treat them exactly alike, but when he told John that he thought first issues were a lot better than later issues, I told him it was bad psychology for our younger son."

"Yes, it is a silly thing, this stamp collecting."

56   On Cowardly Philatelic Writing

Pick up almost any stamp magazine from the last century and your hair will curl at some of the libelous statements made therein. While philatelic politics never came to the stage where duels might be fought, some of the accusations would have called for a meeting on the field of honor a half century earlier. But now the weapons were pen and pencil. The typewriter had not yet come into general use.

A few of the old timers carried on the custom to modern times. Stanley Ashbrook was never one to mince words. If he did not like someone, he did not save his rage just for letters to the object of his scorn. Almost every letter that he wrote screamed for vengeance against the individual. Sometimes, the reason for his anger was a minor slip of the pen in an article the other philatelist had written, or even a mistake in a judgement on an item Ashbrook thought good or bad.

I had a rather extensive correspondence with Ashbrook over the years and when I destroyed the files of forty years with prominent philatelists, prior to moving to Florida, I had a nostalgic time reading his letters. It served no purpose to preserve them; most of the individuals he wrote about had passed on. Of course, the Philatelic Foundation is still with us. Ashbrook went wild when he disagreed with some of their opinions.

Elliott Perry immortalized the name of Henry C. Needham, not only in his conversation and letters, but in his Pat Paragraphs. When that series of his publication was reprinted, all references to the Needham feud were omitted. Needham had "done" Perry out of a commission on the sale of a collection and Perry never forgot it. He accused Needham of being an arch faker, with some truth, stating that Needham had deliberately created fakes for personal gain. (Needham, a millionaire several times over, did not need the money.) Needham wrote the Local section in the Scott Specialized Catalogue, thus making it difficult for dealers to sell genuine ones, because they did not agree with the photos in the catalogue. On Needham's death, the section was entirely done over.

Stephen Rich had a sense of humor that sometimes went

beyond the humorous. In the course of a feud with a lady named Margaret Roselle, he went a bit too far and got himself into trouble with the authorities. Mrs. Roselle was writing a postal history of New Jersey; she was a resident of Lodi, New Jersey. Rich found a stampless cover of Lodi, New York, a long established town. He deleted the "Y" of "N.Y." and skillfully inserted a "J". It caused Mrs. Roselle many lost hours in research, since postal archives showed Lodi, New Jersey as not even existing in stampless days.

She and Rich then had a blistering correspondence, in the course of which Mrs. Roselle suffered a complete physical breakdown, from which she died. But she did not leave philately before she brought formal charges to the postal authorities against Rich for allegedly counterfeiting a U.S. postmark. Rich came within inches of being tried for the offense.

Today, libel laws are such that most letter writers are hesitant to put things on paper which might later be the substance of a lawsuit. And now that we know that so many of the routine letters many of us have written, especially if on philatelic matters to overseas dealers, have been read and held up by the C.I.A., even more circumspection in the future might be indicated.

We don't see too many signed poison pen letters these days, but the anonymous sort of stuff philately went through in its earlier days does exist. It takes a special kind of coward to send an anonymous poison pen letter. He must be a kind of sadist, and his present hobby is no doubt a more mature version of the old juvenile pulling-the-wings-off-flies trick. There is little difference between a mugger approaching a victim from the rear and strangling him, and someone who makes an accusation refusing to dignify it with his name so there can be no defense. Yes, there is a difference in degree of the crime, but the method is still the same.

57   If It Looks Like A Stamp...

*Among the more frequent inquiries a philatelic columnist re-
ceives are those involving letters that have gone through the mails
without bearing valid postage stamps. A variation of this is the
request on the value of a letter that went through the mails without
any stamp. Either of these might be considered a "conversation
piece"—a badly overworked phrase which Main Street folk like to
use when they cannot attribute value to something, but do want to
attribute desirability. The trouble is, people can talk about something for nothing, but that doesn't mean they want to buy it.*

Uncle Sam must be defrauded of thousands of dollars
daily by having to handle mail for which postage has not been
paid. Fraudulent it may be. But we would doubt the fraud
is intended deliberately in other than a few cases.

The facts simply are that there are so many things that look
like a stamp, it is impossible to expect more than three-
quarters of a million employees in 35,000 Post Offices to
remember just which are stamps, and which are not. It is
doubtful if 50 percent of the philatelists can pass this test.

Uncle Sam has issued postage stamps with face value as
high as $100 which are not valid for postage now. (This, I may
say, is exactly why, today, they are worth about $10, even
though they date from 1895.

Certainly it is illegal to use for postage what actually is a
substitute for a stamp. But it would be difficult for the Post
Office to prove intent to defraud in such a case, although,
technically speaking, they would not have to prove intent
since the fraud on the Post Office is obvious.

The facts are that Post Office employees would be unlikely
to suspect a stamp-like seal, etc., that actually might not be
valid for postage, and the letter would complete the trip
without too much notice being directed at it.

Post Office personnel are instructed to watch for mail
which is either not franked at all, incorrectly franked, or
insufficiently franked. Many Post Offices have signs which
read "Watch for underpaid mail." Employees naturally are
conscientious in this regard, yet some pieces of mail do slip
through.

There are thousands of employees in the Post Office whose job each day is to change the slugs in cancelling devices from one day to the next. Some large offices have dozens of cancelling machines; every office has at least one to be changed. The operation must be done perhaps 200,000 times daily from one end of the nation to another.

It is inevitable that in so many operations, a certain number will be incorrectly done. The year 1966 may be inserted upside down, to come out 9961. An incongruous date such as November 32, instead of November 23, will occur. Such incidents are curious but hardly rare, and certainly a piece of mail bearing evidence of this accident will not have any value, for the instances would be multiplied a thousand-fold if examples of it enjoyed any market.

At Christmas time particularly, many mail users, either by eye trouble or hurried confusion, use Christmas seals on their letters. The act is illegal of course, but with our stamps each year outdoing Christmas Seals in religious design, this mistake is more likely to increase than decrease. Although the chances of escaping prosecution are rather large, it is illegal—and it warrants caution.

58 Stamp Swindling...In Three Easy Lessons

Success stories have been written in just about every line of endeavor, including the philatelic, but never before has a confessed stampic swindler boasted of his proclivities to the extent that he desired to write a book about it. And when the swindler numbered murder among his accomplishments, the old success story gag is certainly being given a novel twist.

It is a good many years since this happened, but the files of the A.S.D.A. may include the name of the Krejer brothers of Rochester, New York. They did not go to the Kansas State Penitentiary for the money they owed some of the New York auction houses. They expanded their life of crime with the murder of a motorist whom they picked up in order to rob him of his car.

Stamp dealers began to breathe easier on learning that the Krejer brothers were safely behind bars in Kansas, serving a long term for murder.

The Krejer's philatelic interest went back many years through their exceptional skill at convincing stamp dealers of their honesty, enough to enable them to receive some extraordinarily fine selections of stamps from dealers whose names are household words to us all. Through an elaborate system of offering themselves as references to the suspicious few, and the fact that they were extraordinarily nimble at moving about the country, the philatelic protective bureaus never seemed to be able to catch up with them, and warnings as to their latest aliases always seemed to come just too late. Operating in cities as widely separated as Tulsa, Oklahoma, and Buffalo, New York, or New Orleans, Louisiana, and Cleveland, Ohio, they covered the country quite well.

The attorney for the A.S.D.A. at the time was Harry Citret. Harry had a monthly bulletin of stamp crooks until the Association was advised that offering that service to members might make the Association liable for income taxes. "Tax" was a word not in the vocabulary of the then Executive Secretary.

Mr. Citret had been hot on their trail for months, and through his monthly bulletin no doubt cut their ill-gotten gains to but a fraction of what it might have been had they been allowed to operate without any curbs on their activities. The fact that they had no end of aliases apparently enabled them to work without interference from the Post Office, since the latter seldom troubles to make an investigation unless they receive a dozen or so complaints against one name.

The letter, bearing a neat purple rubber stamped marking, "Censor No. 6", read as follows:

Kansas State Penitentiary

Box 2, Lansing, Kansas

July 29, 1942

Gentlemen:

I am now writing a book on various methods used in defrauding stamp dealers by mail. It also contains various suggestions on how to minimize this loss at little cost.

I am writing you people concerning my book, as you are best informed about my methods and working in the past, and you have the right connections, I believe, to get the book published.

You probably have me listed in your files under any of the following names:

Henry S. Hanson, Arnold H. Bates, St. Louis, Mo., Burton K. Elliot, Cleveland, Ohio; Charles Coleman, Buffalo, NY; Francis B. Johnstone, Joseph Merritt, John Verity, Donald Willard, New Orleans, La.; Douglas van Dusen, Ralph McClain, Indianapolis, Ind.; Philip Pruitt, Lawrence B. Latimer, Moffat Stamp & Coin Co., Louisville, Ky.; Edward Sloane, Memphis, Tenn.; George Sauber, Francis X. Boydan, Sauber, Stamps, Tulsa, Okla.

If you people are able to find a publisher for this book, I shall greatly appreciate it. Trusting to hear from you soon, I remain

Very truly yours,

Joseph V. Krejer

The Krejers did not get a reply from the A.S.D.A., and their letter was taken as an attempt at a little blackmail, conducted from their cell. It is surprising that the Kansas prison authorities did not show any interest in stopping the scheme.

59 "Licenced" to Sell Stamps

Countless books have been written on the subject of the world's first postage stamps. Any stamp collector who does not know that one of Great Britain's gifts to the world was the postage stamp is mightily uninformed on our hobby. Only a slightly fewer number of persons will recall that the inventor was Rowland Hill, later knighted by Queen Victoria, and that the day of issue was May 6, 1840 (although examples improperly used earlier are known).

But how many collectors know that, although the stamps themselves were sold at face value at post offices, the companion Mulready envelope and lettersheet were sold at a small premium, to cover the extra cost of the paper, and so as not to compete unfairly with the establishments scattered over the country which sold sheets of paper and allowed the use of quill and ink for the purpose of writing letters.

And how many are further aware that private businesses were also allowed to sell the postage stamps and the Mulreadies for the convenience of the public, but they were required to have a license to do so.

In the writer's collection of early Great Britain was a Mulready letter sheet addressed to "The Honorable the Commissioners of Her Majesty's Stamp Office, London. "It was an application from One John Kemp, in Folkestone, Kent, for a license. Interesting is the fact that the application was dated May 9, 1840, just three days into the use of the Penny Black. The letter may have been posted the day that it was written, but since May 10 was a Sunday, with most smaller post offices closed, it was not postmarked until the following day, May 11. The next day, as shown by the receiving backstamp, May 12, it reached London.

One may assume that Mr. Kemp, learning on May 6 that postage stamps were then available, sought to buy some for his store at the local post office, and that he was told that he must apply to London for a license. (In the U.K., the word is still spelled "licence".) He lost no time in applying. His letter, on the back of a one penny lettersheet, follows:

"Wishing to sell the Postage Stamps, Covers and envelopes for Letters and finding I cannot do it without a 'Licence' will you be pleased to inform me if I may have one, what the expense will be for a 'Licence', and under what Regulations the 'Licence' is conducted. An early answer will oblige.

Honoured Sirs

Your Humble Servant

John Kemp

Folkstone

May 9, 1840"

At the bottom of the message, Her Majesty's Stamp Office has written: "Refer party to Mr. Colland of Canterbury."

To make certain that Britons will never forget Sir Rowland Hill, at his death he received one honor paid to other famous Britons: burial in Westminster Abbey. His funeral took place there in 1879, attended by some of the greatest dignitaries of the Empire. But he received what was perhaps an even greater honor: his statue, of heroic size, was erected before the head Post Office of the kingdom, just a few steps from St. Paul's in London, where others of Britain's greats are buried.

The statue still stands there today.

60   Maybe a Smile, If Not a Laugh

It was a wise man who remarked that it takes much more exertion to frown than it does to smile. Perhaps it is time once again to leave the serious side of philately, and turn to the part that exercises one's smile muscles.

There were the two stamp dealers who tied in the contest for the world's laziest business man. The judges were undecided as to whom the prize should go, so they asked the two top contenders to state why each felt he should receive it. One explained that he never answered inquiries that came from his ads, and that he never showed up at his office before noon.

The other dealer was asked why he felt he should get the award. "I don't reckon I know why, but if you do decide on me, just put the prize in my pocket."

* * * * *

The psychologist was advising the patient who could not get his mind off his business.

"Night and day, week day and weekend, I can't think of anything else but business. It is ruining my home life with my family."

The doctor advised him to take up stamp collecting. The patient started going to stamp auctions, buying philatelic books, attending stamp clubs, going to stamp shows.

He was back at the doctor's within a year. "I did what you said, but now I can't get my mind off stamps and my business is just about bankrupt. How do I get my mind back on business?"

* * * * *

The wife was scolding her husband for thinking more of his stamps than he did of his marriage.

"Why, I'll bet that you don't even remember what we did on our first anniversary."

"I certainly do," he replied, "and I'll never forget. That was the day that I completed my set of Famous Americans plate number blocks."

* * * * *

Finally, there was the collector who pulled a Rip Van Winkle, and fell asleep for twenty years. On awakening, he picked up the phone, and called his stamp dealer.

"Jim has been dead for ten years," he was told, "and I took over the business. What can I do for you?"

"I want to know the prices on some stamps I may sell if I can get enough for them. What are you paying for a White Plains sheet mint?"

"Anywhere from four thousand dollars up, depending on centering."

"And the fifty cent Zeppelin? I have quite a few singles."

"We bought some yesterday for three thousand dollars each."

"How about sets of Flag Name blocks?"

"They bring about twenty-five hundred dollars each. But how long a list do you have? We're mighty busy here."

"I have about fifty items I want to know about."

"I'm afraid that I can't help you on the phone, but if you cannot come in with your stamps, make a list of them and send it in, and we'll get back to you." "I'll be glad to," said Rip Van Winkle's imitator, "but I have been away for a while. What does it cost now to send a letter?" "The latest first class mail rate is two hundred fifty dollars for a letter, but the rate is going up again next week, so don't wait too long to send that list."

61   Were You A Law Breaker Today?

Uncle Sam's long arm, so the story goes, reaches far to catch the unlucky culprit who breaks his laws. Usually it is best to stay on the safe side and respect the rulings he has set down in order that our country may be a better place to live. Federal laws are respected, and few willingly run counter to it. Yet one still on the statute books is broken daily by millions. I venture to say that even I, at some time during my philatelic career, have broken it.

This law was duly passed by both Houses of Congress of the United States of America in March 1855, and signed by the president. To my knowledge it has never been repealed.

"It shall be unlawful for any postmaster or other person to sell any postage stamp or stamped envelope for any larger sum than indicated upon the face of such postage stamp, or for a larger sum than that charged therefor by the Post Office Department; and any person who shall violate this provision shall be deemed guilty of a misdemeanor, and on conviction thereof, shall be fined in any sum not less than ten nor more than five hundred dollars."

There was a good reason for the law even though there is no reason why it was never repealed.

Stamps were hard to get in the early days of the West. Possession of a stamp enabled anyone to mail a letter at night when the post office was closed or it permitted someone to hand a letter to a friend to mail without worrying about finding a post office open to sell a stamp.

Some postmasters in the West, especially California, attempted to hold stamps for their special friends and even exacted a premium from senders of letters who wanted stamps to take back to the mine fields with them so that they might post letters where post offices did not yet exist. The Act of March 3, 1855 was the result.

62　A Specialty Awaits You

How many collectors know that telegraph stamps were being produced in handy booklets more than a quarter century before Uncle Sam adopted this convenience? Telegraph stamps were distributed for various reasons, but all involved offering possessors a manner in which they might pay for telegrams. The collecting of telegraph stamps in the United States is not as popular today as it was six or eight decades ago, even though the Scott Specialized Catalogue does a very commendable job of listing and pricing them.

But for some reason, Scott has neglected to list telephone stamps, which had a similar background, and a similar mode of distribution. Relatively few people collect them, simply because they are unknown to most collectors, but they can be just as interesting.

A book on British telephone stamps exists, and at the STAMPEX banquet in London in 1983, I had the pleasure of sitting next to the author, who was awarded a prize for his work. The prominent British philatelic writer, Peter Collins, used the occasion to write of British telephone stamps in his 'Cinderella' column in the British magazine 'Stamp Collecting.'

By the 1880s, the place of the telephone in our lives was pretty well established, although few homes could afford one. The cost of installing a phone and maintaining it was quite expensive, and the phone company, to increase its revenues, decided to make the phones in its own offices and exchanges available to the public. There were no pay phones, but the company sold stamps to the public, which would be accepted for calls. Rowland Hill's ideal accounting system, the sale and use of stamps, was extended to the phone system.

The first company to use stamps was the National Telephone Co., headquartered in Glasgow. The general manager, A. R. Bennett, had a stamp designed, and humorously, he suggested that the stamp bear the photo of a Col. Jackson, Chairman of the Board. The suggestion was taken seriously, and the stamps appeared in various denominations picturing Col. Jackson. There was a 1d, 3d, 4d, 6d and 1/-.

On the appearance of the stamps, the public was aghast, accustomed as it was to seeing only the portrait of Queen Victoria on its postage stamps. Although they insisted that use of the Jackson vignette was quite legal, they nevertheless said that they were preparing a new issue, which could not be accused of lese majeste.

After several years, the matter was reopened, and the company insisted that the new stamps were about to appear, but all the while they were endeavoring to dispose of their stocks of the offending ones, by offering them to the public at attractive prices. At the International Exhibitions of 1886 and 1890, Mr. Collins tells us, the stamps were on sale at the company's booth, cancelled to order, no less!

In 1891, the Post Office was losing patience, and pressed its case, but by then two things had happened that made the matter moot: supplies of the old stamps were about gone, and a coin box to permit phone patrons to pay for the calls as they made them had been invented. Something else had happened by then: Col. Jackson was no longer connected with the company.

Canada has also issued telephone stamps, some prepared by the Bell System, and others by individual provinces, including Alberta, Saskatchewan, British Columbia and New Brunswick.

63   The Tiniest Bit Of Postal Stationery

One of the more unusual novelties in postal stationery came about when a cigarette company in New Zealand decided to test its product in 1892, by inserting a prepaid postal card with each pack of cigarettes.

Since the pack of cigarettes did not permit the use of a postal card of normal proportions, Austin Walsh & Co. of Auckland, distributors of Atlas cigarettes, arranged with the post office to manufacture a tiny card, which might well be one of the smallest bits of postal stationery ever put to use.

The card measures one and three quarter inches by three inches, and it bears a half penny stamp, exactly similar in design to New Zealand #P4, but of course without the watermark.

The "front" and reverse of the card are reproduced here:

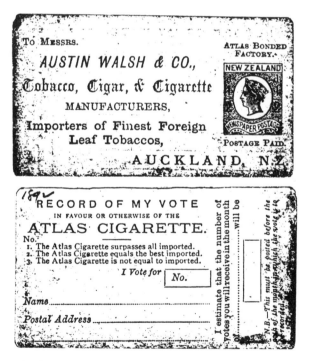

If you look carefully at the stub on the right of the card, you will see that the reverse of the card provides not only for the vote on the merits of their product, but a little lottery was made about it, probably to encourage their buyers to vote. If a prize was to be paid to the winner of the contest, the card says nothing about it.

Curiously, the stamp on the card is a Newspaper stamp, which permitted its being carried at the greatly reduced rate. No doubt permission from postal authorities had to be obtained to permit what is obviously a card, ordinarily subject to the normal rate, to be handled as a newspaper. Here is the further item to consider: how many of these cards must have been lost in the mail, due to their diminutive size?

Does any reader perchance have a used example of this card? And is the card itself unusual? I have no recollection of having seen it before, other than the single specimen before me as I write.

64   Canada's First Stamp Dealer

Who was the first stamp dealer in Canada? In what year did this early philatelist go into business? Where was he located? A positive answer to these three questions will probably never be known, but I have a candidate for the distinction. And if there is anyone who can come up with an earlier one, we would welcome the information.

On my recent trip to London, a friend showed me a letter from Ottawa to London, dated 1866. Unfortunately, the outer envelope was no longer present; it probably was long since destroyed.

It was from a G. Van Felson, who mentioned in the letter he was a soldier in the British Army, stationed in Ottawa. It was addressed to Messrs. Wayte Burnell, 181 High Holborn, in London. Burnell was a very early London stamp dealer, who had done business with Van Felson.

"I am no longer in Quebec," the soldier wrote, "as I am in Ottawa. I need for a collector a 10 pence Canadian stamp which is not available here. I ran an advertisement in an Ottawa City newspaper for one week, and I am now completely out of stamps."

If Burnell could send him a 10 pence Canada (since most of them had been used on outgoing mail, it is understandable why there were none available in Canada), Van Felson told the Londoner he would send him a good number of three pence "old Canada," which were "plentiful," he added.

"Do not pay postage on your letters to me," Van Felson added, "as all my letters come free." (Being on active service, apparently letters to the Ottawa dealer did not need postage stamps, although the soldier added, "I am in the British Civil Service.")

Has any reader ever heard of Van Felson?

Present prices of the stamps mentioned in the letter might be of interest: Canada has only one 10 pence stamp, an imperforate issued in 1855 (Scott 7), cataloguing at $700 in used condition. There is no way of telling which were the three pence stamps that were so plentiful, but they may have been #1 ($350), 4 ($110) both of which were imperforate, or #12 ($275), a perforated stamp. All had a similar design, picturing a beaver in red.

65   To Mail Or Not to Mail?

We haven't kept track of all the old postal regulations—it's impossible to do so—but over the years we have encountered some mighty strange rules, some of which we can't resist revealing here.

If any reader got a letter from a friend in Warsaw asking for a shipment of animal manure, it would have been—and may still be—best that the request be ignored. The import of that product into Poland was definitely forbidden, and any violation of the restriction would find the shipment confiscated.

But before anyone thinks that Poland is somewhat paranoiac about what comes in the mail, readers ought to know that other countries are no less peculiar.

Even more interesting than the prohibition itself would be the reason behind it.   One could send a man's wallet to Afghanistan, but a lady's pocketbook was forbidden. Was it that ladies were not allowed to carry a handbag?

Why should carbon paper have been forbidden in a letter to Bahrain?   Was it to prevent competition with copying machines?   Benin forbade phonograph records, but said nothing about cassette tapes. The bees in Botswana need not have feared competition with foreign hymenoptera so long as the transportation of honey was taboo.   New shoes were admissible into Bulgaria, but not used ones.

Cashew nuts were not allowed in parcels to Yugoslavia, nor binoculars to Turkey.

Just why fly paper was forbidden to South Africa, or soap to Libya, or rubber balloons to Iraq, we cannot even guess. And there was a time when one would have been allowed to send food parcels to Hungary—as long as they did not contain eggplant. Guinea allowed utensils for babyfoods to enter, as long as they did not include a hollow tube exceeding a prescribed length.

One could send bird traps and nets to Egypt, as long as the principal ingredient was not a sticky substance to tangle their feet. Leeches are no longer sold in drugstores as they once were, but even if one had a source for them, last time we checked their export to Cyprus would have been out.

Just why anyone would want to send parasites to West Germany heaven only knows, but we wonder how the authorities stopped them when in the form of headlice or ringworms. Police whistles could not be sent to Guatemala, nor playing cards to Greece.

Finding that postage stamps once could not be sent to Brazil may perhaps explain why an auction shipment we sent there years ago, when we were selling stamps at auction in New York, never arrived. The collector, an American known to us, and above suspicion, assured us that he had signed for and received an envelope without the stamps we had placed in it.

Similarly, silver coins could not be sent to Togo, nor foreign bank notes to Switzerland. (They apparently had enough already from every country in the world.) Soviet Russia objected to any child's game that had anything militaristic about it. (They are the world's greatest peace loving people, we may recall.) And you could send any measuring device to Senegal, as long as the measurements were denominated in the metric system.

When we were well versed in this sort of thing, we knew of two countries that had no exceptions: Surinam and Tristan da Cunha. If it met U.P.U. requirements, as well as postal regulations of the sending country, there were no restrictions to those countries; one could even send manure if one wished.

And one closing admonition: while stamps can be sent to Canada by ordinary or registered mail, better inquire whether they may be sent by insured parcel post. At least a few years ago, this was forbidden; it may still be, and in the event of loss, the sender may be told that he was violating the Canadian law, and has no recourse.

66   The Next Best Thing to A Perfect Crime

Some people say that the perfect crime has never been committed, since the perfect crime is one that no one recognizes as a crime. The perpetrator gets away clean, and no one is the wiser for what has taken place. That may be so, and if it is, in our hobby of philately we had the next best thing to a perfect crime—one that was so skillfully executed that no one knew it had taken place until more than a quarter century later, by which time the guilty party was no longer among the living.

The date was 1872 and the place was the London Stock Exchange. The Exchange's transactions were forwarded by telegraph. The telegraph companies, of which there had been several, had been taken over by the General Post Office in 1870 at the instigation of the British Post Office. In the United States, there also had been many individual companies, but competition and bankruptcy finally reduced their number to the handful that now exist.

A telegraph office was located in the Royal Exchange and the stock brokers wanting to send messages simply took the telegraph forms to the window for acceptance. The charges were paid with postage stamps which were affixed to the telegram itself. Telegrams varied in cost, depending on how many words and to what location they were destined, the rates starting at a shilling for twenty-five words.

There was no way to match up the use of shilling stamps with the number of telegrams sent, since the shilling stamps were also in use for postage purposes. In fact, far more shilling stamps were used postally over the entire United Kingdom than for telegraphic purposes.

Almost nothing is known today, other than the fact that in 1872, counterfeit shilling stamps began to be applied to telegrams.

Whether the stamps had been privately made and sold to users prior to use is not known. Whether there were others in on the scheme to defraud the British Post Office besides the man in charge of the window is not known.

What is known is that in 1872, and well into 1873, the counterfeit stamps were used, and an estimate of the cost to the post office was almost one hundred thousand dollars.

Had it not been for a philatelist, the counterfeiting of the stamps would never have become known, even today, and the perfect crime would have been exactly that.

But in 1898, Charles Nissen, a London stamp dealer, purchased a huge accumulation of old telegrams with thousands of stamps affixed. Although the green shilling stamp of 1872 was still relatively common, the accumulation did warrant soaking and sorting, and Nissen proceeded to do this.

The shilling green of 1872 was an easy stamp to counterfeit. Rather than being engraved, it was printed by the simple process called letter-press.

The counterfeiter had to be a philatelist. In 1872, the shilling green was appearing with its plate number, "5", worked into the design, but soon another plate was brought out with the number "6". The faker was aware of this. His products soon appeared with the changed plate number.

One can fake the design of a stamp, but it is difficult to counterfeit a watermark, since that is placed in the sheet before printing. As a security against counterfeiting, the shilling green was printed on "Spray of Rose" watermarked paper.

Of course, once a telegraph form was canceled, no watermark would be visible. When removed from the telegraph form, however, Nissen found large quantities of unwatermarked stamps, which had never been issued. Even more indicative of the lack of philatelic knowledge on the part of the counterfeiter was the lettering combinations in the corners. The letters used made an impossible combination, which would have given the game away at the time of issue had they been noticed.

In our example here, we see a Stock
Exchange forgery cancelled on July 16, 1872 and still attached to a small piece of telegraph form. But the plate position letters B P make up an impossible lettering combination.

169

It was twenty-six years since the stamps had been used, and Nissen showed the stamps to the authorities and told them of his conclusions.

There was no doubt that the stamps were counterfeit and that someone in the Stock Exchange had been selling fakes and pocketing the money. Scotland Yard had a record of all the Stock Exchange employees who had worked there twenty-six years before, and all those still living were questioned. Some had, of course, died in the meantime and it is presumed that among these was the maker of the fakes.

The stamps are still frequently available and often appear in London auctions. They are not known postally used, and every one that has turned up in the eighty-three years since Nissen discovered them has the familiar postmark of the Stock Exchange.

Was it the perfect Crime? If one leaves it to the person who conceived it, operated it and got away clean with it, we have to agree that it was.

67 Double Your Profit & Pleasure, Part I

One does not have to be an expert at remembering dates to have postal history pay financial dividends that few other philatelic interests make possible. Whether one memorizes them, or looks them up on a handy pocket chart, matters little. The truth simply is that real pay dirt awaits the philatelist who is curious enough to look at more than the stamp on a cover.

An example is a common stamp, Scott #26. Nice covers with #26 can be bought for a half dollar or so. And postmarks of Charleston, S.C. with this stamp are not scarce, for in 1860, Charleston was an important post office, and thousands of letters must have been handled there on December 18.

If you had a letter postmarked with that date, a collector who appreciated the unusual would not think much of it. But if it were two days later — December 20, 1860 — lucky indeed would be the collector of Confederate States covers if he could get it for a couple of hundred dollars or more.

It is the same stamp; it is the same postmark. But on December 20, 1860 South Carolina seceded from the Union. The stamp on the cover might have read United States, but it is actually a United States stamp used in a foreign country, for South Carolina was no longer part of the United States.

One does not have to go back to the last century to boost the value of a common-looking cover. Alaska became a state on January 3, 1959. It had been a territory since October 11, 1867. And postal history collectors love to own covers with postmarks of our fifty states, while they were still territories.

California never was a territory. True, it became part of the United States after the War with Mexico in the 1840s. It considered itself a Republic, and it declared itself independent, and it had its own flag. The "Bear Republic" disappeared on September 9, 1850, when it became a state. Covers postmarked before that date carry a premium. After all, strictly speaking, they were not yet in the United States.

Vermont was an independent nation until it became a state on March 4, 1791. Have you found a letter postmarked 1790 from any town in Vermont? Name your price if you have one. Postal historians have been searching for examples for years. They must exist.

Of course you have heard of Laramie. It is in Wyoming. That is, now it is in Wyoming. When it was in Oregon, it was in the same place it is now. It was an important fort on the Oregon trail, and emigrants on their way west posted their last letters there before risking the Rocky Mountains. There was no state to put in the postmark, so the postmark on the cover shown above reads "Fort Laramie O.R." No one is certain what the "O.R." meant, but it seems to be readily agreed that it meant "Oregon Route".

But, without moving an inch, Fort Laramie moved around from state to state until Wyoming was formed in 1868. In 1863 you can find a neat Fort Laramie postmark, but it was then located in Nebraska — the marking reads Fort Laramie, N.T.

The capital of the State of Washington is Olympia, right? You may be right, but if you see a nice cover with a postmark of Olympia, Ogn., don't think you are seeing things. The fact is that not only was Washington part of Oregon at one time, but so was Idaho, and since Montana was once part of Idaho, that makes Montana at one time part of Oregon Territory.

Louisiana was of course purchased from Napoleon when he was hard up for cash, but the real reason that he sold it was that he knew that if Britain wanted to own it, they could take possession with ease, France being tied up in other parts of the world at the time. But Louisiana did not become a state until May 1, 1812. For years prior to that, it was called Orleans Territory, and there are covers to mark the fact.

172

There is a city at the western end of Lake Erie called Toledo. It is in Ohio? So it is — but not always: It was in Michigan, but it was called Manhattan. During the "undeclared war" between Michigan and Ohio, Ohio seized it and changed its name. To palliate Michigan's hurt feelings, Congress took a chunk of Wisconsin and gave it to Michigan, where it is today called the upper peninsula. And what was in another part of Wisconsin? Fort Snelling, which is now in Minnesota. If you were to find a territorial usage from Manhattan, Michigan or Fort Snelling, Michigan (such as the one above), you could rank that find as one of your more fortunate.

A cover postmarked Richmond,Va. on May 1, 1861 is another desirable item. Virginia at that time was an independent nation, for it had seceded from the Union on April 17, 1861 but it did not join the Confederate States until May 7, 1861. In those three weeks, Virginia was its own country.

If you have two good eyes, a modicum of good common sense ought to start paying cash dividends at the first stamp show you visit. Never forget that you have working for you the lethargy, ineptitude and indifference of the ordinary stamp dealer who regards postal history as a field completely beyond his ken.

Sounds easy? It really is. Especially since, as I mentioned earlier, if you do not have a memory for dates, you can get a handy pocket size chart which has all of this information in it, plus a lot more.

68 Double Your Profit & Pleasure, Part II

One well might call the collecting of postal history a "hobby within a hobby"—with the profit factor possibilities doubled, just the same as the hobbies are. And perhaps the best part about postal history is that while an ample purse is helpful, as in most profitable investments it takes second place to knowledge.

The very common 3-cent rose stamp issued in 1861 (Scott 65) is a good place to begin. Although more than a century old, the stamp (being the ordinary letter rate at the time) was produced in such quantities that even today a fine used example costs but pennies, and even a mint one is available at a nominal price. It also is quite common on original cover, that is, on the envelope on which it was originally used.

Civil War buffs know that the point farthest north where action took place was in St. Albans, Vermont, on October 19, 1864. Knowing that, what a thrill it would be to find a 3-cent 1861 stamp on an envelope postmarked that day in St. Albans —the very day that the Confederates, having gathered in Canada, invaded the United States to loot the banks and obtain much needed funds, after which they retreated back into Canada.

No longer would such an item be worth pennies; as an example of a United States stamp used in a spot occupied by the Confederates, its value and significance would increase a hundredfold or more.

Are you one who remembers dates? If so, postal history is made to order for you. A common stamp on a letter clearly posted before February 28, 1861 from Denver is not from Colorado, as you might think. Denver was then in Kansas, as Colorado did not yet exist, and a Kansas specialist would gladly exchange $50 or so for it, even though the catalogue says that the stamp is worth only a dollar.

As we described in Chapter 67, as the Southern States left the Union in 1860 and 1861, there was a hiatus between the time they seceded and when they joined the Confederacy, the time varying from over two months (as with Texas and Tennessee) to a matter of minutes (North Carolina). It is not very difficult for someone with a mind for dates to remember the calendar of secession, and it is rewarding.

174

Here is another Civil War opportunity. Union prisoners of war in Confederate prisons in many cases were allowed to send letters to family or friends under certain conditions. Sometimes they bore only a Confederate stamp; other times if a Northern stamp was available one might find one of each kind on a cover. This combination is both rare and valuable.

Letters from prisoners of war always would also bear markings showing that the contents had been inspected by a censor.

Here we see an August 5, 1864, cover sent to Virginia by a Confederate soldier held prisoner in a Union prison. The combination is a U.S. 3¢ rose, right, tied by Point Lookout, Maryland cancel and a Confederate States 10¢ Blue "No Frame", Scott 11, left, tied by a Richmond, Virginia cancel. The center marking reads "Prisoner's Letter / EXAMINED".

Whatever one fancies in the way of his own historical interest, a philatelic association can be arranged. Submarines? Naval blockades have been broken by submarines carrying mail. A submarine carrying mail traversed the Panama Canal over a half century ago. Another carrying mail more recently passed under the North Pole.

Do the days of the early West fascinate you? All of the great figures wrote and received letters, Buffalo Bill, James C. Fremont, Annie Oakley, Jesse James. If one can afford to spend a thousand dollars or more, he can buy a genuine letter carried by Pony Express; for twenty or thirty dollars, he can buy a letter carried by Wells, Fargo on a stagecoach.

175

Hot air or gas balloons? They were carrying mail on a regular basis in 1870 and 1871, when Paris was besieged by the Prussians. This letter was carried "par Ballon monte" out of Paris January 8th, 1870. It's final destination, through the regular mails, was St. Petersburg, Russia.

Washington sent a letter by balloon in the 1790s; if it were ever found, its value would be in the thousands of dollars.

For the twelve decades or so during which philately has existed, stamps were routinely removed from their covers, resulting in the scarcity today of such covers. Nowadays any philatelist worthy of the name knows that he should never remove a stamp from an envelope, current letters excepted, unless an experienced philatelist has seen it. Veritable fortunes have been lost through this carelessness.

Just as condition is as important a factor as rarity in the case of stamps, so it is with postal history items. It is far less likely for an entire letter, a century or older, to have come to the present day unscathed and unsoiled, but it is precisely for this reason that when it has done so, its price soars. And there always are plenty of buyers.

In the collecting of stamps off cover, the value of an item is quite readily determined. One simply looks it up in the catalogue, and if the item is perfect, a price of full catalogue or well over catalogue is easily agreed upon. If the condition is poor, the price drops readily, in keeping with its condition. Buyer and seller have access to the catalogue, and there is no trouble in each agreeing on the price.

A doctor we know was connected with the Hadassah Hospital in Jerusalem, which contrary to what may be thought, accepts many Arab cases. In his two years there, he learned the language so that he might interview his Arab patients. The stamp bug bit him while in Israel, and when he came back to this country, he decided to collect not the stamps of Israel, but stamps used in Israel while it was under Turkish suzerainty. (Turkey lost Palestine to a British mandate at the end of World War I, and until then Turkey ran the Palestine Post Office, although many nations had their own agencies where their nationals could pick up and send mail.)

With his knowledge of Arabic, the doctor found that he could visit dealers, and in their stocks of Turkish stamps, find postmarks of towns that were in Palestine. He assembled a collection of Turkish stamps used in Israel that was worth perhaps 50 or 100 times what it cost him, although he had no desire to sell. His plan was to exhibit his collection in Israel, where it would of course be of considerable interest.

A number of Cuban emigres who fled Castro have resumed their collections of that country, using their geographic and historical knowledge of Cuba to their advantage. With its frequent rebellions, civil wars, foreign occupations, all of which were reflected in its postal history, Cuba offers a fertile ground for collecting. (Roger Castro, M.D. of Danbury, Connecticut, assembled a particularly fine collection of Cuba postal history.)

One can just about pick his specialty, and postal history will adapt itself to it. A novice collector accumulating straight postage stamps may never be able to hold his own in a conversation with other philatelists, but if he is smart enough to seek items of postal history, in whatever field he selects he can easily become a top expert, and at the same time build a collection with considerably more equity than he put into it.

69   Mail Swindles and Their Origins

Use of the mails to defraud is nothing new. It is probable that there was a great deal more swindling going on via the mails in the last century than in these times. In many instances, the perpetrator of the fraud enjoyed total immunity from conviction. After all, when the victim entered the deal with dirty hands, he would be most hesitant to scream for the police when he realized he had been swindled.

One favorite stunt was the Spanish prisoner swindle, so named because it had its origin in Spain more than a century ago. In the United States, the prisoner was invariably in Mexico. The letter, so the writer wrote, had been smuggled out of a Mexican prison, where he was serving a long sentence for bank robbery. In the robbery, the loot was gold, varying in value from a puny $10,000 or so to as much as a half million.

The prisoner did not wish to wait until he was released, but there was no one in Mexico whom he could trust. But American citizens were a different matter. He had gotten your name from someone in your town who represented you as a fine, honest upstanding citizen.

For five one hundred dollar bills, sent to him in care of a hotel in the city where he was imprisoned, he would send you a map showing exactly where the bank loot was buried. Yours was the only letter being sent (so the letter read), so the writer implored you to reply, the money to be sent by registered mail.

I just came across a typical Spanish prisoner letter, this one from a Senior Rios who wrote from Barcelona April 24, 1924. The letter was addressed to Milton M. Staples, 1814 Hull, Richmond, Va. It bears the then current red 25 centimos stamp picturing King Alfonso XIII.

The letter reads:

> *"Dear Sir:*
> *Being imprisoned here by bankruptcy I beseech you to help me to obtain a sum of 360,000 dollars I have in America, being necessary to come here to raise the seizure of my luggage paying to the Register of the*

Court the expenses of my trial and recover my port-
manteau containing a secret pocket where I have hid-
den two checks payable to bearer for that sum.

As a reward I will give up to you the third part, viz.
120,000 dollars.

I cannot receive your answer in the prison but you
can forward a cablegram to a person of my confidence
who will deliver it (to) me, addressed as below.

Awaiting your answer to intrust you all my secret,
I only sign now

C.

First of all answer by cable, not by letter.

Jose Rios
Lista Correos 1861
Mahon (Spain)"

Never did these letters solicit a reply by letter, for the Post Office Department was well aware that these prison letters were an invitation to defraud.

Sr. Rios himself was a trusting person; he offered only one third of the hidden money to his intended victim, but there was of course nothing to prevent the person answering from keeping the entire $360,000, rather than just one third of it.

Victims of these swindles had only themselves to blame when they would finally realize that there really was no one to whom a complaint might be addressed. The accomplice in an illicit transaction was not likely to complain to the authorities that his attempted involvement in converting stolen property proved unsuccessful. These letters turn up with such frequency that one must conclude that the scheme brought a steady income to the crooks.

A variation on this Spanish prisoner swindle in all probability netted even more fish in the net. The letter, undated but with a 3¢ stamped envelope postmarked November 3, 1893 was signed "Safe-Thing." Postmarked New York, it was addressed to the Postmaster at Kingston, Washington County, Rhode Island and marked "Personal." Curiously, it did not arrive in Kingston until November 14, the date being in the backstamp.

Of course, the letter was intended to tempt the postmaster, who could sell the stamps over the counter and pocket the money. It is entirely possible that the delay may have been due to investigation by the Post Office inspectors, for with it on a small piece of paper is written "S. A. Dixon, Coenties Slip, New York." (Coenties Slip is a street in lower New York, and the site of a post office many years ago.)

Also enclosed was a Western Union telegraph form, addressed to Mr. Dixon at the address named above. The letter making the proposition was typewritten, reproduced on an early form of mimeograph.

Did the postmaster fall for the trick? He probably did not, but if he did, and if he found out he had been cheated, it was quite unlikely that he would make a complaint...and if he did, to whom would he have made it?

The letter follows:

"Dear Sir:

"I have one hundred thousand two cent postage stamps (face value two thousand dollars), that I will sell to anyone who will not ask questions and who knows enough to keep their mouth shut, for $900, or I will sell fifty thousand for $500.

"These stamps are all in original sheets and are in good condition. "If this proposition strikes you favorably, and you are willing to come to New York, I will appoint a place of safety for our meeting on receipt of the enclosed telegram.

"No insult or insinuation regarding your honesty is intended. So, if you will kindly keep this sacredly confidential whether we trade or not, I assure you it will certainly be appreciated.

"This circular letter has been sent to others, and should you wire me and not receive a reply, you will understand that I have already found a customer.

"Yours respectfully,
Safe-Thing"

70   In Search Of A Wife

One does not ordinarily look upon our stamp magazines as a medium to help a reader find a spouse, but we are indebted to our friend, Bill Hornadge, writing in Australia's Stamp News, for reproducing an advertisement that I must have missed at the time it appeared.

It was in Mekeel's Weekly Stamp News, issue of March 22, 1974. We reproduce it here:

ANNOUNCEMENTS

GENTLEMAN STAMP & COIN DEALER — Seeking wife between 25 to 45. (Not Victorian type). Wants lady who understands and loves the hobbies of stamp and coin collecting and is willing to work with husband in already established 30 year Business. Must like Social life and meeting people. Any Business talents greatly appreciated but not required. Trust and warmth and willingness to make a Happy Life for Both is essential. Businessman Owns Home, Business, nice car, plus excellent position in Government work. Is completely Trustworthy, Reliable and has Excellent Reputation and can furnish highest references if needed. Photograph in your first letter and mine will follow in reply. Address your letter to: STAMP DEALER, Box 1226C, Huntington Park, California 90255.   (41

---

71   A Pioneer Flight That Never Landed

A practical joke, conceived three quarters of a century ago in Wallaceburg, Ontario, has resurfaced to throw Canadian postal history buffs into a tizzy.

It concerned a picture postcard, showing the Wallaceburg Public Library, with an early airplane flying overhead. It was one of those postcards made from actual photographs. It was postmarked Wallaceburg, and the brief message mentioned that the sender had seen the plane. There seemed little doubt that it was authentic.

The date—1911 or 1912, I forget which—was very early for what today we call the "barnstorming pilots". The first carrying of mail in a plane was in February 1911 in India; in the United States, it was on Long Island, New York in September, 1911.

While there was nothing to indicate that a plane carried letters in Wallaceburg, the linkup between a posted illustrated card commemorating the flight was beyond any doubt a "Canadian early".

With my article, I asked if any of our readers would go back to newspapers of the time, and confirm this very early appearance of a plane in Canada. I expressed the hope that there might even have been some carrying of mail...perhaps the very card illustrated. Alas, my hopes were not to be realized.

Frank E. Hamilton, of Palmetto, Florida, is a close personal friend of the Honorable D.J. Trunan, the Mayor of Wallaceburg, Ontario. Mr. Trunan put the local library, as well as a local historian, on the trail. The results have just come to hand.

Sorry to say, the card is a fake. Not only that, but it has already been recorded as a fake, first in postcard circles, and now in the philatelic world.

Deleting some personal news not germane to the story, Mayor Trunan wrote Mr. Hamilton:

"With reference to your letter of 7 February 1984, in regards to the Biplane flying over Wallaceburg with the Wallaceburg Public Library, we have finally come up with some interesting facts.

"As near as we can determine, this photo is an actual FAKE. The reference for this is on Page #17, Greetings from Canada (post card book), whereby it is very distinctly indicated that the airplane picture was glued on the original photo to give the desired effect—interesting!!"

One can only conjecture what the practical joker had in mind many years ago when he performed his little trick.

Was it prompted by local pride, an attempt to show that Wallaceburg recognized the importance of the airplane, and wanted to show that it was not too small to attract this then novel form of transportation?

And when these cards of a non-event were put on sale in Wallaceburg, as apparently was the case, what was the reaction of those who bought? Did they wonder how they happened to miss such an important event in Wallaceburg's history, or did they laugh along with the practical joker?

One thing they could not have known, and that is that many decades later, a philatelist would come across the card and be totally misled into thinking that an enterprising aviator chose Wallaceburg, specifically its library, to launch it into aerophilatelic immortality.

Alas, it was not to be.

72   Hit 'Em Over The Head—
They Still Won't Learn

Some people, even though you hit them over the head with the proverbial baseball bat, just seem to find it impossible to learn from the experiences of others. Of course, it is difficult to counter the multi-million dollar publicity of the USPS. In its zeal to push stamp collecting, it asks the new philatelic mariner to steer a course between Scylla and Charybdis. One hazard to navigation is the encouraging of current mint stamps, and the other is the collecting of the junk stamps that are in stamp packets; stamps which while canceled, have never seen postal use.

We once heard a collector say that the reason dealers preach against buying mint sheets at the post office as an "investment" is that they want to do it themselves, so that the collectors will then have to pay the dealers' price or do without. It is a novel theory.

The facts are otherwise. Dealers are quite willing to let the unwise speculators tie their money up in mint sheets. Then if one in 20 should "go up," which is about the way the ratio works out, the dealers are happy to pay collectors a good premium for their Interphil sheets, their 50 State Flags, or their Space Twins, and say nothing of the vault full of sheets for which they would not even pay face value.

Why invest one's own money when one can profit by someone else's? The dealer is buying up early air mails, Zeppelins, better mint plate blocks, while the post office speculator is buying up mint sheets. Which is the better investment? Why does not the speculator buy up the items most likely to go up and, if he even pretends to be a collector, the items most needed for a collection?

The answer to that is three words, the "face value syndrome."

The face value syndrome hit us broadly in the face some years ago when we were professionally active. A neighbor was buying current mint sheets at the local post office, and his total purchase was approaching a considerable figure. We knew him well enough to remark that we did not know he was a stamp accumulator.

"Oh, yes," he replied. "I have been a philatelist for 10 years now. I have five complete sheets of every commemorative issued in all that time. I have a wonderful collection."

As we said, we knew him well enough to argue the serious defects in his reasoning. "I fear you are an accumulator, not a philatelist, and by the understanding of most, you do not have a collection," we suggested.

We went on to explain that frequently dealers could offer commemorative sheets from as long ago as 1935 at face value or a tiny percentage over. He was not impressed.

We further explained that in 1935, the various commemoratives were issued in smaller quantities than they were now, usually about 23 million or so as against one hundred and fifty million or more. He remained unimpressed.

"What do you think would turn out better," we asked, with what we thought was a clincher, "a stamp issued 40 years ago, printed in very limited numbers, or a stamp issued currently of which several times as many exist?"

The speculator considered a moment, and came up with his studied reply. "I would say that a stamp bought at the post office rather than from a dealer, for Uncle Sam is behind it and no one has made a profit on it."

Of course he was wrong. Uncle Sam loves to sell mint sheets, and he makes far more on them than any dealer. It costs a few dollars per thousand to print stamps, and Uncle Sam enjoys selling them at $290 per thousand. Now there is a mark-up. But it is the old face value syndrome that makes it look like a bargain.

The fact is that the stamps of 1935 are no better a purchase than most of the stamps being issued today. If they have not gone up appreciably in 40 years, they are not likely to take off tomorrow. But the story does show the lack of rationale in the mind of the average speculator.

Look at it another way. No one knows how many collectors there are in the world, but if one puts it at 50 million, it is a generous figure. We do not even know how many there are in this country, but figures from two million to 16 million are thrown around.

Add up the circulation of every stamp publication, and add to it the number of members of every national stamp society, and, forgetting about duplication, of which there will be plenty, one does not reach 250,000. Consider figures for a while!

But when they issue 150,000,000 of a commemorative, and tens of thousands start tucking sheets away to sell in the future, one can assume that the supply is going to last a long, long time, and it does.

It is only when a stamp strikes public fancy and collectors want 10 or 10 hundred sheets of it that one zooms; but even then the price eventually settles back when the profit-takers dump their holdings.

The vaults are full of 50 State Flag mint sheets. We saved every used single of this that came on our mail, and we get a substantial amount of philatelic mail. With never less than 30 or so letters a day, during the six months the 50 State Flag stamp was in Post Offices, less than 300 examples came on our mails. On almost every other commemorative, we receive double or triple.

We received less than 50 of the Interphil souvenir sheet stamps. Yet we know from the numbers sold that these stamps are somewhere. That somewhere is a safe deposit vault, and they are not likely to be rarities, despite what the seers tell us.

Most readers will have heard of the Miner Stamp Company of Wilkes-Barre, Pennsylvania. They publish a mimeographed list subscribed to by thousands of collectors and dealers, with offers of individual stamps, accumulations and sometimes the holdings of entire estates.

One of their offerings was a holding of complete mint sheets, all in select condition, from the period from 1945-60. At the time, the most recent was almost 20 years old; the earliest a third of a century old. The face value of the accumulation was $9,500. It had originally been offered in the weekly list at $8,900. There were no takers, so the lot was offered a second time, now at $8,595, which was almost 10 percent below the original face value. We do not know if it sold at that price, but it is only one common example. And bear this in mind: when Miner offered that mint sheet lot at $8,595, you can bet that this figure includes their profit or his commission. In other words, the owner of the stamps is lucky to come out with even $7,500—or almost 25 percent below face value! And if you are wondering if the few small goodies issued in this period—the Palomar, the Stone, the 5¢ New York air mail—were present, the reply is that they were.

Let's stop a moment and think what this means. Someone invested almost $10,000 over a period of years, 25 and more years ago. Had he put that money in a savings bank, he not only would have his original money, but several thousand dollars in interest. Instead, he was not only out what the money would have earned, but a large portion of his principal—and the dollars he is getting back will buy today about 60 percent what they would have bought when he started.

As a comedian would say, "This is an investment?"

Had he started building a collection in 1945, buying mint or used U.S. stamps, 19th century or the first half of this century, his $9,500 would at the very least have been $20,000 today.

Had he bought items which were in short supply in 1945, like the Columbians, the early air mails, commemorative plate blocks, or Zeppelins, his $9,500 conceivably would bring $35,000 today.

And with such a holding, he would find dealers beating a path to his door. But with those mint sheets, about all he can expect is sympathy. So much for the face value syndrome.

Yes, buying from Uncle Sam does pay dividends—to Uncle Sam!

There is no finer investment in the world than postage stamps. This is a truism, but it presupposes that the investor knows what he is doing. The easiest way to buy stamps is to pay your money through the post office window. No worry about centering, about reperfing, regumming. Your only worry comes years later when you try to sell.

Our message is nothing new. It has been preached for decades. Our stamp writers point the way; dealers who are asked will give the facts. But few will listen. That old devil face value keeps getting in the way.

187

It just goes back to another syndrome, the profit angle. Somehow many people who buy stamps can understand that a grocer, a druggist, or a shoemaker has to do business to earn a living, and they are willing to do their share to help. But since there is so much pleasure attached to everything having to do with stamps, a stamp dealer has no right to make money on his stamps.

Just read how many letters to stamp papers deal with machinations of the big, bad dealers. But such letter writers only give indications of their own bias, since, by and large, the relationship between stamp dealer and stamp collector is a relationship far warmer, far closer than exists between any patron and his source.

Every once in a while we meet someone who burned his fingers in stamp collecting, and he will proclaim to us in words large enough for everyone to hear, "Stamp collecting is a racket."

And whenever we hear those words, we are tempted to reply (and we sometimes do), "You are right...to those who tried to make a racket out of it."

73 Modern Fancy Cancels

You might think that Uncle Sam is heartily in favor of all of his nephews and nieces making as much money as they can. After all, why shouldn't he welcome it, when he is a silent partner in all of their ventures?

But as the song says, it ain't necessarily so. He may collect taxes on illegal betting, and demand his share of the profit if you operate a clandestine still, but there are some places where he draws the line. One of them is finding a loophole in the postal regulations that puts money in your pocket, even though it does not take money out of his. In fact, even if it means more money for him, he is not going to sit by and let someone else profit by a postal regulation, no matter how legal it may be.

Incredible? Read on, brother.

Let us go back to 1928: the nation then boasted far more fourth class post offices than it does today. (As roads got better, and farmers could afford automobiles instead of horses and carriages, many small offices have been closed, for rather obvious reasons.)

Many of these offices found business hard to get. The idea of keeping them open was to enable the farmers to get needed supplies from the mail order house, rather than to make it easier for him to send occasional letters. But incoming mail did not help the "take home" pay of the fourth class postmasters. Their pay depended on the business they did, especially outgoing mail. If they cancelled $1.18 worth of stamps on outgoing mail, they got to keep the entire $1.18. If they built that up to $2.36, they doubled their take.

Sounds fine, doesn't it? But it had its drawbacks. If their outgoing mail exceeded $1,500 per year, they were no longer fourth class, and their remuneration (as a second class office) was based on entirely different considerations. The trick, therefore, to making money out of being a fourth class postmaster was to attract outgoing mail, and thus build up one's income...but not too much.

We don't know who conceived the idea of getting collectors of postmarks to have letters forwarded from small offices for that reason, but a study of an extensive collection of these by examining the dates might shed light on it. Perhaps it was

Appleton, Wisconsin, which while not a fourth class office, did point the way. The Appleton postmaster, tired of using the drab, uninteresting postmark Uncle Sam had given him, came up with a pictorial marking. It showed an apple with the letters "T O N" across the fruit. Appleton may or may not have been the instigator, but it was an early one.

Henton, Illinois, a tiny town (and a fourth class office) possibly picked up the idea from Appleton. The Postmaster apparently let collectors know that he would be glad to cancel covers sent to him with a pictorial postmark, showing a hen — with those same letters, "T O N" added to the picture. The fat was in the fire, and towns in all parts of the country went in for pictorial postmarks, especially those with descriptive names that lent themselves to illustration.

Chicken, Alaska got into the act, as did Bear, Arkansas, Old Glory, Texas, and Wheeling, West Virginia. By late 1928, literally hundreds of tiny towns were cancelling covers with an incredible series of cancels. If the town name did not lend itself to being the subject of a pictorial cancel, various holidays were used to justify them. On Washington's birthday, a cancel portraying the Father of our Country was used; Santa Claus held forth on Christmas, Trees on Arbor Day, and Firecrackers on July fourth.

The tiny town of Ed, Kentucky, which boasted the shortest Post Office name in the country, was probably the most extensive source of modern fancy cancels. It really didn't have the shortest name, as there were other names composed of two letters, but at least no office had a shorter name. Ed really went to town, and today dozens and dozens of different Ed markings are known. Almost every holiday in the year was memorialized; historical events were commemorated on proper dates; even nursery rhymes such as "three men in a tub" or children's poems found themselves on covers. Fraternal emblems were celebrated by many towns, including the Masons, the Oddfellows, and the Elks.

Collecting modern fancy cancels soon engulfed the hobby, and as the postmasters discovered this easy source of revenue, they let the stamp magazines know what was available, and collectors flocked to send their covers to the different offices.

Fourth class postmasters raked in the funds. Today a collection of these will disclose certain names that repeat themselves over and over, names like Floyd Shockley, a banker, of Indianapolis, or Robert F. Molitor, of Cleveland. There were many others. Thanks to people like these, who ordered dozens of each type of fancy cancel, they are available to us today at modest prices.

But, as always happens in philately, the fakers soon took the field. All one needed was a plain white envelope, some postage stamps, and a set of rubber stamps portraying various animals or objects. Such a set was standard fare for children, and could be bought at almost any toy store. The fake covers started appearing wholesale, devoid of any post office name or date, but with the stamps cancelled by a sailboat, an airplane, or a horse.

Collectors soon learned to protect themselves, and the fourth class postmasters welcomed the insurance method chosen. The registry fee was only a dime in 1928-1929, and the postage rate was but two cents. By affixing twelve cents in stamps to a cover, they could request registry, and thus assure themselves of not only the handstamp of the sending office, date and all, but a backstamp of the receiving office as well. One reason Uncle Sam discontinued putting a receiving backstamp on registered mail was to break up this fancy cancel craze. Even today the only modern fancy cancel covers that are sought are those that were registered; only a very unwise collector would put any money into one bearing ordinary postage. The secret of course was that while anyone could fake the fancy cancels, it was infinitely more difficult (as well as illegal) to fake the registry handstamps of the two post offices involved.

Uncle Sam was a long time taking steps to curb the fancy cancel doings. As the depression deepened, more and more offices went into the business. Cleveland and Indianapolis continued to be the principal markets for such covers. Examine a collection of them today and note how many are addressed to collectors in these two cities. Every state in the Union had more than a few post offices producing fancy cancels on registered covers for collectors.

It was about 1933 or 1934 that Uncle Sam began to look with disfavor on the practice, although there was not too much that could be done about it. Some students insist that the Post Office actually forbade the use of home-made cancels, thus ending the scheme, but if this is so, the writer has never seen such a regulation. Home-made cancels have always been used to a minor extent; they are still occasionally used today. During World War II, Salem, Oregon, (thanks to a postal employee, Edwin J. Payne) used a very fancy "V for Victory" cancel.

Perhaps the collecting world was so submerged in a surfeit of fancy registered covers that collectors stopped sending for them, for the market for them virtually ceased to exist. Collections came on the market which dealers bought simply for the stamps. The writer in the late 1930s and early 1940s soaked thousands of them simply to get used copies of such stamps as the Norse, the Ericssons, the Walloons and others. At the time they were used, such stamps had little premium value, and were often used on philatelic mail. But with the great philatelic boom that began with F.D.R.'s election to the presidency, such commemoratives began a steady ascent in price.

One very early use of a fancy pictorial cancel in mass production occurred in Houston, Texas, in June 1928. The Democrats held their nominating convention in Houston that year; they nominated Alfred E. Smith of New York, who lost in the election to Herbert Hoover.

We don't know today who conceived the idea, but some enterprising Democrat, recalling the "kicking mule" cancels of a half century before, realized that the donkey was the Democrat emblem. Literally thousands of covers posted from Houston during the Convention received not only the regular Houston postmark, but multiple applications of a "kicking mule" and the words, "He's in Houston." Apparently the marking was applied in the Post Office, for it is inconceivable that politicians would have access to such a vast quantity of mail.

By the mid-1930s the practice had all but vanished. Towns with names like Forty-Four, Pennsylvania, and Ninety-Six,

South Carolina, went back to conventional postal markings and dropped their pictorial numerals. Silver Bell, Arizona, and Rising Star, Texas, put their canceling devices aside, as did Young America, Indiana, and Horse Shoe, West Virginia.

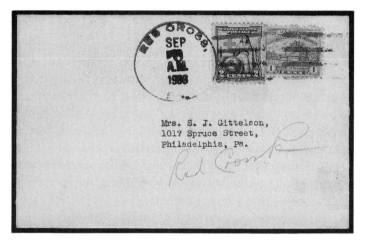

Although fancy pictorial cancels may no longer be provided, even today one can build a nice collection of unusual town names. The Red Cross, Pa. post office no longer exists, but there are many other cancel candidates still out there, often with stamps that make a good match.

74 Touring Canadian Philately

It is almost a century since Canada, emerging on the world scene as a nation flexing its muscles, began to object to United States citizens assuming that they — and they alone — were Americans.

As we know today, their campaign was not too successful, even though Mexico joined in the attempt.

Of course, they were correct. Canadians and Mexicans are as much Americans as any other citizen of the New World, but it is well nigh impossible to fight the use of a word which by now has been so well accepted. However, in reference to Canadian susceptibilities, many residents south of Canada attempted to find a single word that might describe themselves, without adopting the misleading word "American". For a time, it was thought that they had found the word.

The name was USONA — United States of North America. Several important newspapers in the States accepted the word, and recommended that it be used. Citizens of Usona might be called Usonians. Things pertaining to Usona would be called Usonian.

Today, the name Usona is just about forgotten, and almost permanently buried. To my knowledge, it lingers on in a section of land near Pleasantville, N.Y., in Westchester County, New York. The unincorporated cluster of homes call themselves Usonia. It is doubtful if a single person there knows the origin of the word, but it is a reminder that a century ago there were United States citizens who realized that their country had no justification in usurping the name "Americans".

* * * * *

Where does the paper on which Canadian stamps are printed come from?

As most Canadians know, their nation's virtually inexhaustible stand of timber (now that replanting takes place as it is harvested) makes the paper industry one of Canada's most important. It is important enough to have been the subject for philatelic representation. (See Scott Nos. 316, 362)

A Canadian paper manufacturer, Abitibi, one of the largest such businesses in the world, for years made the paper used for stamps by Canada Post. It was the only firm in Canada, it has been stated, making such paper acceptable for stamps. However, Abitibi told Canada Post that it was not profitable for the company to continue, and it asked if it might give up the contract. Canada Post turned to the firm of Harrison, in Britain, which still exports much of the paper used for Canada's stamps.

* * * * *

According to Direct Marketing, a magazine devoted to direct mail advertising, Canadians may see their post office engaged in working for various mail order firms.

Some time ago, Victor G. Baker, of Montreal, wrote as follows in "Direct Marketing":

"C.P.C. (Canada Post Corporation) hopes to take the post office more deeply into the mail order business, making greater use of their 5,000 vehicles across the country, 8,200 branch operations, large storage and warehouse space, and good communications. One postal official said they have the fastest-growing courier service in the country. Now they want to get involved in mail order. 'We're talking to firms who sell refrigerators, stoves and similar items through mail order, and we want to see if we can do it for them on a fee basis. We'd train inside postal workers and sorters to handle the business'."

* * * * *

Collectors who have studied the postal history of the Gold Rush of 1898 have known for a long time that the international boundary between Canada and the United States was not a cause for concern.

In the first place, no one quite knew where the boundary was, and persons were more concerned with finding gold than in knowing which nation ruled the soil on which one stood. Ownership of land was not quite the issue that it was in the California gold rush a half century earlier.

Perhaps the greatest effect was on postal arrangements. Post Offices on either side of the more or less non-existent border simply found it convenient to recognize the stamps of the other nation. Covers with United States stamps were postmarked at Canadian offices, and the opposite was equally true.

195

75   So You Want to Be A Dealer?

Among the most frequent types of letters sent to this column are those from collectors who have decided that they would like to become dealers. The number of these letters does not surprise us. If a hobby brings pleasure to an amateur, how much more pleasant it would be to continue to make a living from it.

No sensible dealer is against competition, for the more stamp dealers there are, the more collectors there are. Cities with several dealers have the most stamp clubs, and the greatest numbers of collectors. Cities without a major stamp store generally are philatelic deserts.

A Mekeel's Stamp News reader in North Carolina has been collecting stamps for some years, and asks advice on how he can get into stamp dealing, in order to make a little extra money to buy stamps. He has a fine collection of stamps, he says, and a few hundred dollars in capital. He even owns a small postal card size mimeograph machine. He would like us to give, in print, some good tips on getting into the stamp business with the hope of making it profitable.

It almost seems that every collector at one time or another has similar ideas, and it is true that most successful dealers have at one time been collectors, but success in the stamp business takes a great deal more than a collection and a mimeograph machine. No one could ever count the number of collectors in this country who are trying to make money from their hobby. But there are statistics as to those who do not make the grade.

Trade research among dealers reveals some interesting figures. It is a fact that it is easy to sell fine stamps, but it is very difficult to buy them at a price that permits profitable resale. At any given moment, by far the greatest number of rare and valuable stamps is in collections, and not in dealers' stocks. The dealer in the long run has to make it attractive enough to induce the collector to part with his stamps.

All this talk of cartels, rigged prices, fake pricings, etc. is mostly nonsense. Prices can be rigged on new issues, or stamps in plentiful supply, but when a stamp is so scarce that all dealers seek to buy it at once, the fortunate collector holds the key.

The cost of advertising to make one's presence known must be another consideration of business. The several hundred dollars that our friend has may not last long. Classified ads are, of course, less expensive than display, but not always as effective.

Most collectors already have their regular sources for stamps, and if they are pleased, they may have no necessity to try a newcomer who is completely unknown to them. One of the most frequently used ways in which business is enticed from one's competitors is to offer stamps at lower prices. This could attract the price-shopper, of whom there are many, but once one's initial stock is sold, replacement at similar low prices would be impossible. One could make the promise of better service, prompt filling of orders, or a gift with each purchase, but this is no different from what every newcomer is promising.

We do have advice for our North Carolina friend, but it may not be what he wants to hear. Sometimes, writers of letters of this sort want encouragement, and want to be told that the pot of gold supposedly at the rainbow's end is a good deal closer if one embarks on the trail of philatelic professionalism to seek it. Talk to any of today's top dealers, and you will find out how many years they put in 60 to 80 hours a week getting started. You will find that not only they, but their wives and children put in long hours doing monotonous labor that had to be done. You will find occasionally that credit losses from dishonest collectors often had them at the point of discontinuance.

What advice for our friend? That advice is to learn as much as he can about his hobby, so that if he does make the break and decide to hang out his shingle, he will have the most necessary ingredient of success in the stamp business. That ingredient is not the ability to write a catchy ad, nor is it a wonderful collection, nor a great deal of capital. We have seen collectors possessed of any or all of these attributes who did not last a year in stamps.

That necessary ingredient is knowledge. It is the desire to learn as much as there is about one's proposed line of work. It means study of the stamp literature. It means owning a stamp catalogue. It need not even be the most recent. But it does mean using the catalogue, especially the introduction, which most collectors do not even notice. It is a liberal education in itself, answering the hundreds of questions that many dealers today are constantly asking, not even aware that the replies are at arm's length.

And it means reading the many books on the hobby. Your public library should have several of them.

But one of the easiest ways to learn about the product one plans to sell is through at least one subscription to a weekly stamp newspaper. There are several available, and every one is to be recommended.

An individual copy of one of our weeklies can be as little as the cost of a stamp to mail a letter. With a subscription, one gets the news of the hobby from every country in the world. He learns of meetings of stamp clubs, of exhibitions and of stamp conventions.

It also is likely that whatever the types of stamps in which one wishes to specialize, there is already a society existing which concentrates on that country, or issue, or activity.

Your favorite dealer will be glad to tell you of the society or magazine best suited for you, and perhaps to propose you for membership in it, or to help you with a subscription. Only when you join with other collectors in this way will philately bring you the success that you hope to achieve.

Appendix: Knowledge Versus Stamps

One of the most competent philatelists of this or any other generation was the late Herbert Bloch, writer, dealer, collector and all-around expert. Once while he spoke at a stamp club, Bloch said "collectors should start buying a library before they buy their first stamps." That advice will never be taken literally, but as most advanced collectors know, knowledge of what one plans to buy is the certain way to know what to do before it is bought.

I can think of only one other hobby that has the tremendous backdrop of the written word available at modest cost. That hobby is photography. The large number of magazines devoted to photography line entire shelves in shops offering publications for sale. Perhaps philately is second to photography to this extent, but photography does not begin to endow those who read its publications with the wide expanse of learning one can get from stamp magazines.

Hundreds of our most competent philatelic writers are putting their philatelic studies, many developed after a lifetime of effort, into stamp magazines. Many larger studies are published in books at the expense of the writer and sold far below the cost of publication.

The mystery is that with the number of stamp collectors reputed to exist (perhaps 2,000,000 eliminating those who buy commemoratives at post offices thinking that it is an "investment"), no stamp magazine can boast a circulation of even 70,000.

Perhaps some reader of this book might want to subscribe to a stamp magazine. I can recommend all of the following publications to readers. Only addresses are given, and not subscription costs, since these prices may change during the lifetime of this book. Readers are invited to write the magazine of their choice for their current subscription rates. There is little duplication of news and features in these magazines, so subscriptions to as many as the collector can afford are recommended.

Mekeel's Weekly Stamp News P.O. Box 5050, White Plains, NY 10602

Stamps Weekly, 85 Canisteo St., Hornell, NY 14843

Linn's Weekly Stamp News, P.O. Box 35, Sidney, OH 45365

Global Stamp News, P.O. Box 97, Sidney, OH 45365

Stamp Collector, P.O. Box 10, Albany, OR 97321

U.S. Stamps (Quarterly), 10660 Barkley Ln., Shawnee Mission, KS 66212

Canadian Stamp News, 103 Lakeshore Rd., #202, St. Catharines, Ont. L2N 2TG, Canada

Stamp Wholesaler (Dealers only), P.O. Box 706, Albany, OR 97321

* * * * *

Another of philately's finest attributes is the large number of societies devoted to any one of the many specialties collectors prefer. The following groups welcome new members; all have regularly appearing, commendable publications. Write for membership details.

American First Day Cover Society, Tom Stillman, Box 590970, San Francisco, CA 94159

U.S. Philatelic Classics Society, Michael C. O'Reilly, Box 1131, Huntsville AL 35807

Bureau Issues Ass'n., David G. Lee, Box 2641, Reston, VA 22090

American Topical Ass'n., P.O. Box 630, Johnstown, PA 15907

American Air Mail Society, Dan Barber, Box 23055, Lansing MI 48909

Postal Stationery Society, 212 Mecherle Dr., Bloomington, IL 51701

U.S. Cancellation Society, Tom Stanton, 2109 Alice Ave., #2, Oxon Hill, MD 20745

Postal History Society, 8207 Daren Court, Pikesville Md 21208

Confederate Stamp Alliance, Richard L. Calhoun, 1749 W. Gold Rd., #366, Mt. Prospect, IL 60056

Writers Unit (for writers), George Griffenhagen, 2501 Drexel St., Vienna, VA 22180-6906

Precancel Society, Arthur Damm, Pine Manor #3, 8215 Pine Road, Philadelphia, PA 19111

American Revenuer, Bruce Miller, 701 So. 1st Ave., #332, Arcadia, CA, 91006

War Cover Club, Chris Kulpinski, Box 464-F, Feasterville PA 19047

* * * * *

There also are countless opportunities to join a local stamp club in your vicinity, to attend meetings or to receive their publications and attend their exhibits. Prominent local clubs may be found in most major cities, including Portland (Ore.), Los Angeles, Chicago, Washington D.C., Boston, St. Louis, Phoenix, Kansas City, Cleveland, Baltimore, Philadelphia; Montreal, Toronto, Vancouver, Omaha, San Francisco, Sacramento, Dallas, Oklahoma City, Tulsa, Tucson, Houston, and Hollywood (Fla.).

The largest national society is the American Philatelic Society, P.O. Box 8000, State College, PA 16803. A letter to the Secretary will bring you information on most local and national stamp clubs, as well as on societies that operate statewide.

Some of the clubs mentioned above have extensive philatelic libraries and some even own their own buildings. Special attention must be given to one of the oldest and largest clubs of all, the Collectors' Club of New York, 22 East 35th Street, New York, NY 10016.

One final word to readers: while this book is copyrighted, any stamp club or publication wishing to use any part of it may do so gratis, and without asking permission, as long as a credit line is given "by courtesy of the author, Herman Herst, Jr., and the publisher, Mekeel's Weekly Stamp News."